IT'S A
MEANINGFUL LIFE

VIKING
ARKANA

IT'S A MEANINGFUL LIFE

it just takes practice

BO LOZOFF

VIKING ARKANA

A LARK PRODUCTION

VIKING
Published by the Penguin Group
Penguin Putnam Inc., 375 Hudson Street,
New York, New York 10014, U.S.A.
Penguin Books Ltd, 27 Wrights Lane, London W8 5TZ, England
Penguin Books Australia Ltd, Ringwood, Victoria, Australia
Penguin Books Canada Ltd, 10 Alcorn Avenue,
Toronto, Ontario, Canada M4V 3B2
Penguin Books (N.Z.) Ltd, 182-190 Wairau Road,
Auckland 10, New Zealand

Penguin Books Ltd, Registered Offices:
Harmondsworth, Middlesex, England

First published in 2000 by Viking Penguin,
a member of Penguin Putnam Inc.

1   3   5   7   9   10   8   6   4   2

Grateful acknowledgment is made for permission to reprint
excerpts from the following copyrighted works:
"Spanish Pipe Dream" by John Prine. © 1971 (renewed) Walden
Music, Inc. and Sour Grapes Music. All rights o/b/o Walden Music,
Inc., administered by WB Music Corp. All rights reserved. Used by
permission of Warner Bros. Publications U.S., Inc., Miami, Florida.
"Buckets of Rain" by Bob Dylan. Copyright © 1973, 1974 by Ram's
Horn Music. All rights reserved. International copyright secured.
Reprinted by permission.

CIP data available.

This book is printed on acid-free paper. ∞

Printed in the United States of America
Set in Adobe Garamond
Designed by Betty Lew

For Sita, my co-conspirator

in the Great Charade

Acknowledgments

Hats off to Robin Dellabough, Lisa Di Mona, and Karen Watts at Lark Productions for envisioning this book long before I did. And hearty thanks to my editor, Janet Goldstein, at Viking/Arkana, for stretching the usual ways of producing a book in order to make this whole process a spiritual practice right from the start.

My family and friends at Kindness House took on a lot of extra work to afford me the time to work on this book. I love and appreciate them all. My son Josh, especially, poured his heart into compiling much of this material for nearly a year. Anyone who benefits from this book can thank him first.

And of course, to the saints and sages of all times and places, whose presence and energy inspire my every breath, I bow low and beg forgiveness for any ignorance or vanity seeping through in these pages. *Jaya!* Victory to us all.

Contents

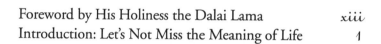

Foreword by His Holiness the Dalai Lama   *xiii*

Introduction: Let's Not Miss the Meaning of Life   1

PART ONE: THE INNER JOURNEY OF COMMUNION

CREATING A PERSONAL SPIRITUAL PRACTICE 13

Waking Up from the American Dream   25
    Practice: Clarifying Your Motivation   30

Spirituality Is Not Optional   35
    Practice: Classic Breath-Centered Meditation   40

You Can Do Hard   49
    Practice: Vow Practice   56

It's Not the Top, It's the Climb   59
    Practice: Facing Fears   64

The Coal Miner's Faith   67
    Practice: "Anything That Can Happen" Mantra   70

Lucky Breaks and Fractures   73
    Practice: Mantras for Everyday Life   76

Our Cosmic Safety Net   82
    Practice: Prayer   87

Take Off the Bumper Stickers   92
    Practice: A Prayer of Humility   98

But Enough About Me   100
    Practice: An Exercise in Seeing   103

It Always Gets Back to Kindness   106
    Practice: Setting the Stage for a Life of
    Lovingkindness   110

❀

PART TWO: THE OUTER PATH TOWARD COMMUNITY

PRACTICING SERVICE   117

Becoming Civilized   127
    Practice: Civilizing Your World   131

Chicken Little Was Right   135
    Practice: Values Exercise   139

The Big Activism   142
    Practice: Living Simply   148

A House Too Small May Be a Blessing   151
    Practice: Sacred Reading   155

What Are We Thinking?   160
    Practice: A Television Vow   166

The Gospel of Following Bliss 168
Practice: Stopping 172

Mistaken Identity 175
Practice: Work/Life Vision Quest 180

One for All, All for One 185
Practice: The Breath of Life 190

. . . The Other Tastes Salt 193
Practice: Daily Marriage Vows 202

The Fortress of Anger 203
Practice: Working with Anger 209

A Mensch Is a Mensch, Big or Small 212
Practice: Taking Inventory 217

Fix Your La-Z-Boy 219
Practice: Working with Your Hands 225

Success by Failure 228
Practice: A Day of Silence 233

Honest Truth and Honest Fiction 237
Practice: Talking Circle—
Opening Honesty to Truth 242

A Time to Speak 246
Practice: Talking Circle—Discerning
Versus Judging 252

Every Mother's Child 254
Practice: Radical Goodwill 260

Afterword: Keeping It Simple 263
Saints, Sages, and Sacred Texts 268
Recommended Resources 277
Index 281

Foreword

I believe that human nature is fundamentally gentle and creative and that it is important for us to recognize this. If we examine the nature of our lives, we find that from the moment of birth until we die, human affection plays a crucial role in ensuring not only that we feel satisfied, but even that we survive. As social animals, we human beings not only depend on each other's support simply to live, but also have a deep-seated desire to communicate with one another, to express our feelings and share our experiences. On the one hand, our need to live together, like members of any family, requires that we show each other tolerance and mutual support. On the other, our diversity is a source of strength and creativity.

In recent times, civilization has made many advances, but we continue to be troubled by problems because of our undue emphasis solely on material development. We have become so engrossed in its pursuit that, almost without knowing it, we have neglected to foster the most basic human needs for love, kindness, cooperation and caring. And yet the development of human society is based entirely on people helping each other. If we lose this essential humanity, what is the point of pursuing only material improvement?

Because the very purpose of life is to be happy, it is important to discover what will bring about the greatest degree of happiness. Our experiences, whether pleasant or miserable, tend to be either mental or physical. Generally, it is the mind that exerts the greatest influence on most of us. Therefore, we should devote our most serious efforts to bringing about mental peace. And in my own limited experience I have found that the greatest degree of inner tranquility comes from the development of love and compassion. The more we care for the happiness of others, the greater is our own sense of well-being. Cultivating a close, warm-hearted feeling for others automatically puts the mind at ease. This helps remove whatever fears or insecurities we may have and gives us the strength to cope with any obstacles we encounter. It is the ultimate source of success in life.

At every level of society from the family up to international relations, the key to a happier and more successful world is the growth of compassion. We do not need to become religious, nor do we need to believe in an ideology. All that is necessary is for each of us to develop our good human qualities.

In this book Bo Lozoff elaborates on these themes. He explains how if we wish to improve the world, we can best start by improving ourselves and enhancing our own innate positive qualities. Despite the despair and cynicism we may see around us, if we make the effort we can transform this precious opportunity into a meaningful life. Amongst the advice the book contains are explanations of the ancient meditative practices recommended by saints and sages, but the author does not neglect down-to-earth suggestions, like simply turning off the television more often, for creating peace and quiet in our lives. This book deals with profound issues in a simple and accessible way. I am confident that anyone of any faith or none can benefit from the universal ideas and realistic advice it contains for improving their own life and the life of the world.

His Holiness, The Dalai Lama

December 2, 1999

Introduction:
Let's Not Miss the Meaning of Life

You and I live in an age when the ordinary seems extraordinary: to take time to watch the sun rise, to enjoy a peaceful cup of tea while listening to music, to eat breakfast or dinner with all the members of our family together at one time (and actually enjoy each other's company). Such simple, human moments are romanticized in commercials for their nostalgia value because they have become so rare today.

And we live in an age when the extraordinary seems ordinary: a relentless pace that would bring Alexander the Great to his knees; a level of materialism and creature comforts that would exceed Cleopatra's wildest dreams; a degree of self-absorption that would make Narcissus blush. Tens of millions of us who can't keep up, or who become understandably confused or depressed, are prescribed powerful drugs to help us fall back into place. This is not just extraordinary, it is incredible.

In our era, even ancient spiritual practices may be used not so much for touching the sacred but for reducing stress so that we can keep up a truly soul-destructive, frenetic level of activity. Americans, for example, turn to disciplines like meditation or yoga more often through the advice of their doctors than through the teachings of sages.

When we dare to slow down and ask ourselves some probing questions, how well do our answers satisfy us? Are we deeply fulfilled? Do we feel our lives have a clear sense of purpose? Do we see our place in the great scheme of things? Do we have confidence in the future of our society? Most of us are certainly not lazy; we expend a tremendous amount of effort in many directions. But toward what ends?

> It is as if a king had sent you to a country to carry out one special, specific task. You go to the country and you perform a hundred other tasks, but if you have not performed the task you were sent for, it is as if you have performed nothing at all. So man has come into the world for a particular task, and that is his purpose. If he doesn't perform it, he will have done nothing.
>
> —Jalāl al-Dīn ar-Rumi (thirteenth-century mystical poet), *Table Talk*

What "particular task" have we come into the world to accomplish? Given the diversity of the world's philosophical and spiritual traditions, you might assume there would be many conflicting answers to this question, but actually that is not the case. The great traditions agree on the most fundamental ideas, such as are described in Hinduism's *Sanatana Dharma*:

1. Something sacred, truly holy, and incomprehensible does exist.

2. This sacred reality can be touched directly by each of us, in our depths.

3. The quest to touch that reality is the primary purpose of life. If we do not touch the sacred, we will "have done nothing."

Yet many of us feel hard-pressed to attend to anything beyond Rumi's "hundred other tasks" which compete for our attention. Nearly every minute of our time may revolve around job and mortgage, bills and debts, personal ambitions and family problems, with an occasional expensive, exhausting vacation thrown in for diversion. And that's considered the *good* life. We have come to think that we have no alternatives. What used to be called the fast lane has taken over our whole highway, and many of us are whizzing right by the ageless spiritual truths and practices that could bring profound meaning and joy into our daily lives. The purpose of this book is to help revitalize and integrate those spiritual treasures into our daily lives.

If we search outside ourselves for the meaning of life, we tend never to find it. But if we center ourselves and look for meaning *in* life, it's always waiting for us, right here in the present moment. And I don't mean self-indulgent contemporary notions of the present moment, like "If I had my life to live over, I'd wear more purple" or "Life is uncertain, so eat dessert first." A deep spiritual life is not merely about "seizing the day" for self-centered gratification. Something more profound is available to us, a spiritual power and freedom that we can barely imagine from an egocentric perspective. We are much deeper than we usually let on.

Spiritual states are objectively real, not merely wishful thinking or personal perceptions. When my heart opens and your heart opens, we do not experience different things. Our personalities and circumstances are left way behind, and we experience the One Great Compassion that has always existed and always will. Some may call it Christ Consciousness, and others *Sat-chit-ananda*. When my mind clears and your mind clears, we do not see different things. We see the One Living Spirit of all creation, the dazzling divine light that connects and enlivens all beings equally. Styles and symbols and languages may express these experiences in countless ways, but the transcendent realities themselves do not change.

And neither do the big truths of human accountability. Each of us is called upon to choose good over evil, love over hate, generosity over selfishness, time and time again. And each of us will reap the consequences of our choices. Neither era nor culture nor popular sentiment can alter these basic truths. As Psalm 100 intones, "His truth endures to all generations." And elsewhere in the Old Testament: "I am Truth. I cannot vary."

We are free to ignore or reject the spiritual laws of the universe, but we cannot render them ineffective. The perennial message of the sages is that if we heed these laws, we will thrive spiritually. If we violate them—going against what the Eastern traditions call Dharma or Tao or, in Judeo-Christian terms, choosing Mammon over God—we will wither spiritually, no matter what degree of fame, fortune, or power we may attain.

Human history is no more than an ongoing narration of this wondrous drama, and you and I are not bit players. According to the wise ones, there are no bit players. Each of us is set upon a hero's path, each of us is sent by the king to perform the "particular task" of struggling through countless illusions and compelling temptations to become as holy as is our birthright.

So each of us has an essential choice to make: Do we trust a growing modern notion that life is chaotic, random, and morally neutral, with no greater significance than whatever we ascribe to it? *Life's a bitch and then you die. He who dies with the most toys wins.* Or do we choose to trust the compass of the sages and saints—that life has profound meaning, and each one of us can touch the Divine. If so, it makes sense to familiarize ourselves with some of the classic maps and rules of the road, and make sure we are on a path we believe is a good one.

Many years ago, my wife, Sita, and I chose to take our chances with the teachings of the sages and saints. The more we studied and practiced, the more we noticed that every great religion or wisdom tradition revolved around the same two main principles, one dealing with internal spirituality and the other dealing with external spirituality:

1. The internal principle says that each of us, in silence and solitude, can touch and eventually merge into the Divine Essence deep within us. We could call this principle *Communion*. Religions may differ on their names or ideas for what it is that we commune with, but they all agree that through diligence and earnestness, we can commune with the Highest Force imaginable, whatever we may wish to call it.

2. The external principle all the religions share is a simple ethic about how we are to regard others. We are instructed to love and respect all of creation, to be forgiving and compassionate and generous, and to dedicate our lives to the common good rather than merely to personal success. A universal word to describe this principle

is *Community.* We are to have a spirit of Community as the primary motivation to guide our
lives.

While Rumi's "one task" may seem to suggest that perhaps
Communion is the only important goal, the great faiths
have consistently made it clear that our internal work and
external work are interdependent and never fully separable.
Without loving and caring for others, most of us stand little chance of communing with God, no matter how many
years we may spend in silent prayer. Service to God's creation is a potent form of prayer. Communion and Community may be seen as the common twofold prescription
written by the great religions as the means to fulfill our
"one task" of God-realization.

Great figures like Jesus, Buddha, Muhammad, Teresa of
Avila, Ramakrishna, Ba'al Shem Tov, and countless others
have left behind a wealth of teachings, stories, practices,
and examples that show us how to balance the principles of
Communion and Community so we don't get completely
lost in the confusing maze of worldly life. Such practical
guidance abounds; we are not left alone to figure out how
to live spiritually.

Sita and I have been so stirred and changed by what we
have discovered in these spiritual teachings and practices
that we have never regretted leaving the fast lane for the
vast lane. Our lives continue to unfold with a power and
grace far beyond anything we could have arranged through
our own limited imaginations.

We certainly never would have dreamed that our life's
work would unfold from the unlikely beginnings of the
Prison-Ashram Project, which we began in 1973 with our
friend and first mentor, Ram Dass. After sending free

copies of his landmark book, *Be Here Now,* into prison libraries around the country, Ram Dass began to receive correspondence from prisoners who were hungry for practical spiritual advice in the prison environment. At that time, I had a few family members in prison and felt a growing need to offer myself in some way into that realm of pain, fear, and suffering.

When Ram Dass and I discovered our mutual interests, we had what seemed like a small idea: to extend open, interfaith spiritual friendship to prisoners. Ram Dass has long since moved on in other directions, but the Prison-Ashram Project we co-founded is now probably the oldest and largest such resource in the world.

Many of the hundred or so letters we receive every day from prisoners and their families include statements like "I was just about ready to give up on myself when I received your books. You literally saved my life." Sita and I never dreamed that we would see the inside of hundreds of prisons around the world, but it has been a great privilege that has deepened us in ways we could never describe.

After many years of focusing primarily on prison work, we created the Human Kindness Foundation as an umbrella organization for other projects and interests as well. My lecture and workshop schedule takes me around the world to talk with people about subjects as diverse as the state of society, prison reform, marriage and child-raising, interfaith spirituality, nonprofit careers, sacred stories, and anything else that seems worthwhile to discuss with other concerned human beings.

A more recent project of the foundation is the Interfaith Order of Communion and Community, which provides common practices and precepts for several hundred participants spread around the globe (about 70 percent in prison). They all engage in some sort of local community service, meditate with us at prearranged times, and let us know how they're doing each month.

In the early 1990s, our rising mail load—upward of fifty letters each day—made it clear that our work could no longer be done as a mom-and-pop operation from the little shed-office in our backyard. Sita and I now live at Kindness House, a spiritual community of ten to fifteen people who run the Human Kindness Foundation and all its projects. Kindness House is our full-scale application of the principles of Communion and Community. The third principle that guides our lifestyle here is simple living, as our response to the personal and planetary problems created by excess consumerism and debt.

At Kindness House, we begin and end each day with silent spiritual practice (meditating, praying, reading, doing yoga, walking in nature). We construct all our own buildings, grow much of our diet, mill trees for lumber, build a lot of our furniture, and operate tractors and forklifts and all sorts of fun things that figure into an operation like this. Carpentry gives me something especially precious. For Sita, it's having her hands in the soil of our garden, or making beautiful stained-glass windows for our small, passive-solar cabins.

The steady stream of visitors who come to share our community life for a few days or weeks or months is another gift. As one of our residents has said, "The world comes to Kindness House." When I gaze around our dinner grace circle and see guests from Australia, India, Germany, or elsewhere holding the tattooed hand of a reformed murderer who spent many years in brutal prisons, in turn joining hands with my son and daughter-in-law, old rock-and-roll musicians, visiting meditation teachers or monks or nuns, retired schoolteachers, corporate dropouts, wealthy donors, or indigent wanderers, I experience an almost ecstatic sense of gratitude. Gazing around the circle at such a bizarre mix of human beings, I can almost hear Jesus cheering at the top of his lungs, "Now *this* is what I had in mind!"

I am always struck by how strongly visitors seem to be affected by our simple daily practices—group meditation first thing each morning, then a brief spiritual reading led by one person; silence until breakfast; then a focused workday of joyful service, not chatting while we work or during meal preparation; little things like that. Small, enjoyable details to us who live here, but sometimes life-changing for the people who visit. It became clear that a book focused on such accessible practices and ideas may be timely for many people who feel that their lives are either spinning out of control or simply not quite satisfying.

This book is a sharing of nearly thirty-five years of study, practice, and hands-on experimentation with interfaith spiritual teachings in my own family's life. It is also a criticism of many of our mainstream culture's current views or styles, especially the way consumerism has come to dominate every sphere of human life. As the monk Sujata said in his book *Beginning to See,* "The Buddha did not come on Earth to tell us he thought the world was moving in the right direction."

I believe in a joyous and fulfilling personal life. I also deeply believe that our civilization is in serious trouble. To present one without the balance of the other would be misleading. So here you have both. I hope that the social criticisms do not overwhelm your optimism and that the spiritual messages do not lead you to focus on your inner work to the exclusion of the suffering and dysfunction around you.

There is much work to do, both inner and outer, and we can plunge into it with great determination and spirit.

Plunging into the inner work is the subject of Part One of this book—The Inner Journey of Communion. Plunging into the outer work is the business of Part Two—The Outer Path Toward Community. The introductions to each part convey the essential understanding of the ideas in all the chapters that follow. The chapters begin with questions I hear fairly frequently, and end with specific practices that enable the reader to *do* something with the information presented. This is very important to me, because as Wang Yang Ming said ages ago, "To know and not to do, is in fact not to know."

The same essential meaningfulness calls us all, albeit often in a whisper—a "still, small voice" that may be drowned out by the noises of everyday survival. But that whisper keeps calling and calling until it begins to break through in the dead of the night, or following a painful transition or loss, or some other time when the worldly noise is silenced just long enough for us to hear what we need to hear.

And when that happens, we may find little signs, new friends, unexpected resources, or something else out of the blue that gives us the opportunity to experience life in a deeper and more holy way than we had ever imagined we could. I hope this book is one of those unexpected gifts in your life—right on time, right on target, reinforcing the inner whisperings you can no longer ignore.

• Part One •

———————— ❧ ————————

THE INNER JOURNEY OF

COMMUNION

Creating a Personal Spiritual Practice

Life's meaning does not need to be invented or deduced or conjectured anew in each age. It can be experienced if we but begin to follow the bread crumbs dropped by those who have traveled the road before us. Countless spiritual pilgrims have felt the longings you and I feel, have encountered the obstacles you and I encounter, have devoted themselves to truth as you and I say we wish to do. It is a great reassurance to pick up their writings or teachings and begin adapting them to the particulars of our own lives. We are not so alone as we may think.

One of my favorite lines from the Christian gospels is, "He marks the sparrow's fall." The Hindu Mahabharata says the same thing: "I salute Lord Krishna, to whom nothing is impossible, nothing unknown, and nothing unbearable." Both these passages suggest not only God's omniscience but also God's concern and caring. If God knows and cares about everything, then it stands to reason that everything counts. Our lives do have meaning. Life is basically good underneath all the struggle or confusion we may face. Everything fits.

But in our daily swirl of events, passions, deadlines, pressures, and crises, what is the best way to remember that life is good, or that everything fits? Remember the old joke? A fellow walks up to a streetcorner musician on the street of Manhattan and asks, "Excuse me, sir, how do I get to Carnegie Hall?" The man sternly replies, "Practice!" and walks away.

One of the most essential teachings of all the saints and sages is to perform serious, diligent spiritual practice. Even the most sincere reading and study are not enough to effect genuine transformation. Nor is "just being natural" or "going with the flow."

Of all the world's spiritual traditions, Taoism especially emphasizes naturalness and flow, allowing things to be just as they are. Yet even Lao-Tzu, the founder of Taoism, weighs in solidly on the side of practice:

> Don't think you can attain total awareness and whole enlightenment without proper discipline and practice.
> This is egomania.
> Appropriate rituals channel your emotions and life energy toward the light. Without the discipline to practice them, you will tumble constantly backward into darkness.
> —Lao-Tzu, *Hau Hu Ching*

We must be willing to do the spiritual work that gradually brings us into communion with what is eternal and divine within us. Our whole lives become a spiritual experiment in the laboratory of the real world.

Practice is the means by which we try to tame the mind and body to be our servants rather than our masters. The actual techniques passed on through the great traditions are usually not complex or sophisticated; they are generally simple, repetitive activities that gradually move our minds closer and closer to Communion. Universal spiritual practices include breathing, meditating, reading sacred texts, doing yoga, walking, praying, repeating mantras and vows. I also describe other kinds of practices that may seem less traditional, such as working with your hands or writing down some of your basic values.

I know how terribly hard it can be for us to change our lives in major ways. I know how easy it is to be cynical about trying yet one more round of ideas or practices or vows; we've failed so many times. But on our way toward becoming free from all habitual behavior, it is often necessary to first replace bad habits with good ones. The habit of spiritual practice—especially at the beginning of each day—can remind us of who we are and what we wish our lives to be about. If we are sitting at our altar every morning and evening dissolving all our identities—as Joseph Campbell put it, not knowing what our name is or how much money we owe or what kind of car we drive—then we only have about sixteen hours at a time to screw up our lives. Vices and bad habits can't flourish as easily if we're cleaning the slate every sixteen hours. It's a great help.

It is also useful to remember that we practice not merely to make our lives immediately more enjoyable. We do not even practice to become deeper, but rather to become more aware of our depth. We already are deep; we just keep forgetting it. As our balance shifts, and our "default mode" becomes generally spiritual rather than worldly, we develop an unforced equanimity that helps us breeze effortlessly through circumstances that may at one time have brought us misery.

A WORLD OF PRACTICES

Practices can also help us become more mindful about specific issues such as eating, exercise, and talking. For example, we may say, "I'm not going to talk about anybody outside of his or her presence." That may be only one tiny aspect of mindfulness. But the practice will help us develop that aspect of mindfulness. We'll catch ourselves if we start talking about someone. The same with taking a day of silence and hearing in our minds all the things we would have said during that day. Or practicing "mindful work" by not chatting about unrelated topics while we are working. Such deliberateness is at the core of our spiritual work because we want to have conscious choice over what we do.

Fasting is another spiritual practice many of us find useful. Fasting quiets us. It takes away out outermost shell of energy because we're not feeding it. The second or third day of a fast, we quiet down a lot. When I'm fasting, I make it a point not to trivialize the practice by carping about how much I love pizza or how much I'm dying for ice cream. When people fast at Kindness House, I may recommend that they help make their favorite meals for the rest of us. In other words, when we fast, the point is not to avoid the struggle, but rather to look at the whole of it. We try to see the dignity of fasting: *I'm just not eating. Of course, the food smells great. But I'm fasting. No big deal.*

Another food practice is a "no-seconds" vow. We may often take two more slices of pizza than we are hungry for just because it tastes so good. I do that! An occasional no-seconds vow for a month at a time helps curb such gluttony. You put on your plate however much you feel is enough for that meal, and then you abstain from any second portions. When you start to go back for more food, you remember, "Whoops, I'm on a no-seconds vow."

Practices such as these help us become more deliberate, and deliberateness helps us develop more equanimity. It is a wonderful sense of freedom to feel equanimity when privation or disappointment come our way. Having a fender bender on your way to an important meeting, arriving home with someone else's dry-cleaning, being stranded overnight in an airport terminal because of airline incompetence—as trivial as such examples may seem in the context of the sacred journey to God, they can actually take years off our lives when we lack the equanimity to accept them with a good sense of humor.

There is also a long tradition of using physical exercise as spiritual practice. Tibetan Sherpas have hiked barefoot up the world's highest mountains. Native American runners traversed enormous valleys and plains with trancelike ease. Modern-day marathon competitors speak of the "Zen of jogging."

The extraordinary prowess made possible by focusing mind, body, and spirit toward one task is no longer a controversial idea. But it does require self-discipline. If we allow the mind to race around while we're exercising, or if we exercise while listening to a motivational tape or chatting with friends, then it's just physical exercise. What turns any mundane activity into spiritual practice is to focus entirely on that activity and, for the most part, to do it in a quiet, receptive state of mind. Especially in the case of physical exercise, people are often surprised at how much more they get out of it physically when they approach it spiritually.

THE PRACTICE OF SPIRITUAL PRACTICE

We are always beginners on the spiritual journey. We don't need complex or esoteric practices; we certainly don't need an enormous changing variety of them. We do need to make spirituality the hub around which the wheel of our daily life turns. To work deeply and naturally, spiritual practices require time, commitment, and patience. Choose some that you are drawn to, do them every day, and you will see significant changes in your life. This isn't arguable or hypothetical. It is tried-and-true ancient wisdom.

There are many levels of spiritual practice. I have attended numerous formal retreats led by swamis, teachers, monks, and masters, and I have also done many personal solo retreats, turning only inward for guidance. I have traveled across the ocean to sit silently in the presence of a holy woman. I have given up sex, music, writing, and teaching for as long as three years at a time in order to see more clearly my deliberate relationship to each of those parts of my life. I have spent as long as two months in total silence in order to break free from habitual patterns of speech.

But the ultimate proving ground of all practice is our day-to-day life. We can't escape that supreme crucible of our existence. In the seventies I could come out of a month-long retreat feeling calm, compassionate, and wise, and then attend a big family Thanksgiving dinner that would reduce me to an uptight, blabbering idiot within a couple of hours. Such experiences are so common in the American meditation community that they even have a name: postretreat letdown.

Not that retreats and training with masters are valueless. I recommend such serious exploration to anyone who has an inclination and the proper circumstances to do it. Tremendous gains can sometimes be made. But if your present life situation precludes long retreats, residential training, or spiritual pilgrimages, you can still venture deeply into your personal spiritual garden by integrating some classic perspectives and practices into your day-to-day life.

Spiritual progress cannot be measured like educational or physical progress. Watching a video about Mother Teresa while you are in a humble and open state of mind may affect your life more powerfully than a two-week meditation retreat (see Practice on page 110). A personal catharsis in the midst of a solo weekend retreat might change you more than a month in an ashram. Consciously giving up all annoyance and road rage as you encounter rude or bad drivers may transform your relationships more quickly than a trip to India.

Wherever you are, in whatever circumstances you find yourself, you are in an ideal position to perform spiritual practice. But you must give it its due. I recommend that if you wish to explore a spiritual practice, take a vow to perform that practice for at least one month, at the same time every day, before evaluating whether you like it or whether it's "working" in any way. The Vow Practice on page 56 gives tips for how to go about that.

It is also important to have a correct view about spiritual practice right from the beginning. The point of such practice is not to escape pressures or get our minds off our problems, although either may happen as a welcome side effect. The real purpose of spiritual practice is to strengthen our presence of mind right here and now. Spiritual practice helps us handle what Zorba the Greek called "the full catastrophe"—anything that comes our way in the rip-roaring roller coaster of life.

It's not about changing the event itself—although miracles do seem to happen sometimes as we develop faith and awareness—but about staying in the moment of reality, remembering that even this moment belongs in our spiritual journey. As we become able to face danger or conflicts without getting lost in fear and denial, we have the opportunity to play the hero of our dramas rather than their victim. Life dramas can take an almost playful turn when, as Buddhist teacher Pema Chodron puts it, "your curiosity becomes stronger than your fears."

For that reason, many of these practices can be done during the course of the day, not only at some special time like meditation or yoga. For example, the best (and most difficult) time to work on anger is when we are getting angry, so I've included a Practice on page 208 to do in that very moment. Nothing outside can prevent us from doing spiritual practice. I have learned that lesson well from my thousands of prison friends who choose to develop awareness and compassion in some of the noisiest, angriest, most brutal environments on earth. Their amazing persistence has transformed my life.

In the pages that follow, I describe simple, accessible practices that can help you do productive spiritual work. My own studies and experimentation have led to a style of practice that suits my nature, just as your studies and experimentation will lead to a style that suits yours. But all of us need to touch some balance of mind, body, and spirit with our practices. All of us need to balance the mystical and the pragmatic.

As time goes by, as our hearts open and our vision clears,

we discover there is nothing really to balance: mind, body, and spirit are one; the mystical and the pragmatic are one. Our lives become a seamless whole, and every moment becomes our conscious practice. We accept life and life accepts us, and the fears, worries, and internal bickering of a lifetime fall away. Getting there is not always easy. But the joy and gratitude inherent in this spiritual awakening surpass any other kind of payoff life could possibly offer. It is truly the Grand Relief.

And beyond even the Grand Relief, the ultimate purpose of all spiritual practice is to reach a state of uninterrupted Communion, a state in which no difference exists between "my will" and "Thy will," or indeed between the self and God. "I and the Father are One," Jesus said (John 10:30). The Sikh religion intones, "Now are for us no entanglements or snares, nor a bit of egoism left. Now is all distance annulled, nor are curtains drawn between us. Thou art mine, I Thine" (Adi Granth M.5). In Communion beyond ego, it is God who lives in us and through us, and does a much better job of our lives than we could ever have imagined possible.

My friend and fellow writer Rabbi Rami Shapiro provides a wonderful way of framing this idea:

> It rained heavily during the night, and the street is thick with mud. I walked to the Bet Midrash [House of Learning] this morning and stopped to watch a group of little children playing with the mud. Oblivious to the damp, they made dozens of mud figures: houses, animals, towers. From their talk, it was clear that they imagined an identity for each. They gave the figures names and told their stories.

For a while, the mud figures took on an independent existence. But they were all just mud. Mud was their source and mud was their substance. From the perspective of the children, their mud creations had separate selves. From the mud's point of view, it is clear such independence was an illusion—the creations were all just mud.

It is the same with us and God. "Adonai alone is in heaven above and on earth below, there is none else" (Deuteronomy 4:39). There is none else, meaning there is nothing else in heaven or on earth but God.

Can this be? When I look at the world, I do not see God. I see trees of various kinds, people of all types, houses, fields, lakes, cows, horses, chickens, and on and on. In this I am like the children at play, seeing real figures and not simply mud.

Where in all this is God? The question itself is misleading. God is not "in" this; God *is* this.

Think carefully about what I have said. It is the key to all the secrets of life.

—Rabbi Rami Shapiro, *Open Secrets*

What is that key—that God alone exists? If that is so, then I do not exist as a separate self. Realization of this nonexistence of the self is a core teaching of every religion, and the goal of all Communion practices. That's why I prefer the word "realization" rather than "enlightenment." "Enlightenment" sounds like something we attain or achieve, which is not the case. We simply realize what has always been true and real.

Let's say you are wearing a blue shirt and you walk around saying, "I wish I had a blue shirt on, I wish I had a blue shirt on." I approach you and say, "Hey, look down. You do have a blue shirt on." The moment you look down and see your shirt, you realize the truth and become happy. It did not become true at that moment; it had been true all day long. But because it was an unrealized truth, you had not been enjoying it.

You and I look around and we see a diverse creation. My guru, Neem Karoli Baba, looked around and said, "Everywhere I look, all I see is God. That's why I'm always honoring everything." Hence the term "God-realization." Simply realizing that everything is God. The scales fall from our eyes and we see the truth, which has always been true. We can find such references in every tradition, indicating a real experience, a real state of being, not just a belief or metaphor or philosophy but a genuine Communion with an ultimate fullness that comes only when we empty ourselves totally.

As many of us have noticed, such total God-realization is not wholly within our conscious reach, nor can we confine it to a formula based on the number, type, or longevity of our practices. God has mysterious cards up his sleeve. We are told there is a certain amount of grace involved. One person plugs along at meditation for forty years without much headway, whereas another may reach a stage of enlightenment ten minutes into the first sitting.

But that doesn't mean our practices are unrelated to such awakening. Many years ago I accompanied the late Israeli Rabbi Shlomo Carlebach as his guitarist. One evening he told the crowd, "Full experiences of God can never be planned or achieved. They are spontaneous moments of grace, almost accidental." Later that night when we were

alone, I asked him "Rabbi, if God-realization is just accidental, why do we work so hard doing all these spiritual
practices?" His reply: "To be as accident-prone as possible!"

Holy men and holy women, the most "accident-prone"
spiritual pilgrims, laugh a lot and seem to take paradoxes
such as these in stride, without worrying about rational answers or understandings. It is mainly their insights and also
their practices that fill the following pages, so that you and
I may learn to laugh like they do.

Waking Up from the American Dream

I feel as if I've got all the right ingredients in place for a satisfying, enjoyable life. But they're not adding up in some essential way. I still feel a sense of yearning for more, an absence of real joy. What am I missing?

The Buddhist tradition emphasizes an element of spiritual living translated as "right view." The idea of right view, like the old saying "Don't miss the forest for the trees," reminds us that no matter how many good components we may have for a fulfilling life, those components must also fit into a bigger picture with which our individual lives are in harmony. In other words, if we come to some idea of what life in the largest sense is about, then we may begin to understand why or how our personal life falls short of fulfillment. We may even be surprised to see that we are not so unfulfilled as we had thought. Much of our vague yearning and sense of incompleteness may be due to wrong views shaped by modern media and unrealistic expectations.

Be all you can be. Just do it! Climb every mountain. Dare to dream. These bumper-sticker philosophies of our day sound appealing on the surface, but they are tied to a consumer model of life's purpose that never brings us the wholehearted satisfaction we inwardly crave, because consumerism—while promising satisfaction at every turn—relies on our never being satisfied. Underneath its ingeniously wholesome images and compelling slogans, this life view is about selling products, nothing more.

The two chief forces of consumer marketing are desire and fear. *Eat this, drink this, do this, drive this, and you will be happy. Take this pill to avoid pain.* Meanwhile, the spiritual teachings of the world point to desire and fear as the two great shackles of human existence, the two biggest barriers to our natural joy.

Of course, we all experience desire and fear. From the time we are infants, desire for what may please us and fear of what may hurt us are important navigational systems. Their existence is not the problem; it's how we respond to them that counts, how (or whether) we integrate them into a more mature navigational system guided by right view.

The sophistication and power of modern advertising and "infotainment," and the consequent globalization of consumer values—what many analysts have begun to call Earth, Incorporated—have made it harder and harder to integrate our natural desire and fear into a mature navigational system, because consumerism relies on ceaseless desires and fears. Helena Norberg-Hodge, author of *Ancient Futures: Learning from Ladakh,* makes the intriguing observation that the entire world, at present, is dominated by a mentality that used to be associated with American teenage boys smoking cigarettes and riding motorcycles in black leather jackets.

Even if you and I have simplified our lives and have adopted alternative values, it would be foolish to assume we are not influenced by the same blitz of messages and perspectives that bombard the mainstream culture with the lure of materialism, superficiality, and sense gratification. Let's face it: consumerism has taken over the world because it works! When I take the first bite of a Dairy Queen cone dipped in melted chocolate—ah, delicious! I'm a happy man. But is there a cone in the world big enough to keep me happy for more than a few minutes?

Earth, Incorporated, exhorts us to pursue that ultimate cone with all our might (and dollars). Clever marketing has even convinced many of us that it is unhealthy not to satisfy our desires and fears. But when desire goes unchecked, it will eventually tempt us toward selfish or harmful or even criminal behavior in order to fulfill its object. When fear dominates us, we will eventually withdraw from others, or try to avoid life's natural ups and downs in unnatural ways.

Living in servitude to our desires and fears is living like the dogs who pursue a plywood rabbit around the race track. Not only do they never get to catch it, but even if they did, it's not really a rabbit, it's only painted plywood. They just run around that track all their lives for nothing. This is a truth many of us discover only when we attain everything we thought we wanted, and still feel incomplete and unsatisfied.

Keeping our heads on straight in this day and age requires conscious and persistent effort. One way to look at our pursuit of an appropriate state of happiness is to break it down into two parts:

1. What is my biggest view of life and my place in it? That is, what are my primary values?
2. What steps or behaviors are necessary to bring my daily existence into harmony with that view?

The gap between our sincere values and our actual behavior is the source of all self-hatred. And self-hatred is the antithesis of personal happiness. So it makes sense to ask these questions at the beginning of each day, or at least fairly often, and to spare no effort in bringing our behavior into line with our values. Nothing is more important. We will not find happiness while we are divided between the two.

I have also found that scrupulous self-honesty helps a great deal in integrating our fears and desires into a mature sense of happiness. For example, many of us, including me, have had some measure of problems with drugs or alcohol. When I lecture now at recovery centers, I try to point out that one part of me would love to smoke a joint at that very moment, or drink an ice-cold beer in a frosted mug. If I pretended that I hated being high and had no nostalgic pulls toward smoking or drinking, I would be at much greater risk of backsliding, because I would be living in denial. When I talk about these things, you should see the relief on the faces of recovering addicts who had been wasting a lot of energy trying to pretend there was nothing they missed about their old ways.

We can acknowledge our desires while at the same time not indulging in them. In fact, this is the essence of free will. In my life, drugs and alcohol come with too many strings attached, so I choose not to fulfill my desires for them. We cannot avoid some of the desires that come into our minds, but we can choose to fulfill them or not. Spiritual practices contribute greatly to the strength of our free will, so that we may choose to respond to our desires and fears in keeping with our deepest values.

The Bhagavad Gita tells us that only the person who possesses self-control over desires and fears is on the road to happiness. Another requirement for being on that road to happiness, also expressed in the Gita, is giving up trying to control things outside ourselves. You know the feeling: going through each day like a bowler who has already released his ball but is leaning this way and that way, waving his hands toward a strike, shouting and nearly falling onto the floor in gyrations that have no power whatsoever over the ball or the pins. How often do we wave and shout and gyrate over things outside our control? *I've got to find a parking space.* Desire. *No, no, don't let this be a flu coming on; I don't have time this week for the flu!* Fear.

True happiness, or what we may call joy, is internal, not external. It does not result from finding parking spaces or avoiding illnesses. It comes from taking responsibility for the things under our control and learning to embrace even the unpleasant things that are not under our control. Superficial happiness is the illusory pot of gold at the end of the rainbow, while joy is the whole rainbow right in front of our eyes.

Another difference between superficial happiness and real joy is that joy can coexist with sorrow. Vietnamese Buddhist teacher Thich Nhat Hanh has used the expressions "joyful sorrow" and "sorrowful joy." When we are feeling down for any reason, we remind ourselves that life is still essentially good underneath whatever is troubling us, so our sorrow does not necessarily go away, but exists with an undercurrent that is positive and grateful. Joyful sorrow. Conversely, when we are feeling wonderful, it is good to remember how much suffering and struggle continue to go on all around us, so that we may always bear compassion in our hearts for those who do not share our blessings. Sorrowful joy.

To be sorrowful with no sliver of joy is to be blind to the big picture, the transcendent and unified. To be happy with no heartfelt sorrow is to be blind to the little picture, the suffering and despair among the people and nations of the world.

But does it work to search for these states of joyful sorrow or sorrowful joy in the first place? Is that how they are found? The happiest people I have ever met have been people who gave up their search for happiness and just lived according to their highest beliefs and biggest view.

Michelangelo said that a sculptor doesn't create anything; he sees something of beauty within a block of stone, and then begins to chip away at everything that hides it. If it is true that real happiness and joy reside within us, then we simply need to keep chipping away at whatever it is that tempts us toward a smaller, more self-centered view of life.

> Ah, the Joy, to discover there is no happiness to be found in the world!
>
> —Wei Wu Wei

A Practice: CLARIFYING YOUR MOTIVATION

As basic as it may sound, very few of us take even a few seconds each morning to remind ourselves of who we are, what we believe in, or what we hope to do with our lives on this particular day. The mind is a powerful repository of the messages it takes in. If we begin each day by reminding ourselves of our right view and our best intentions, we will gradually find it easier to see through the contradictory messages and temptations we encounter during the rest of the day.

Script directors talk about a "throughline"—a theme that moves from the beginning to the end of an entire script, even though many auxiliary events and subthemes may occur along the way. Clarifying our motivation is one practical way of keeping a spiritual throughline all day long.

THE BIG CLARIFICATION

To catch your mind when it is most open and quiet, do a clarification before you settle into all the nooks and crannies of your personality for the day. Either while you're still lying in bed or at the beginning of your morning meditation session, train yourself to bring thoughts such as the following into your awareness. Select just two or three at the most, and give each one time to sink in to your deepest motivational centers.

I am a seeker of truth on a spiritual journey. I believe life has sacred meaning and purpose.

May my behavior today express my deepest beliefs.

May I approach each and every task today with quiet impeccability.

May I be a simple, humble, kind presence on the earth today.

May I see the Divine Nature in all beings today.

May I be grateful today to those who came before me, and may I make the roads smoother for those who will travel them after me.

May I leave each place at least a little better than I found it today.

May I truly cherish this day, knowing that it may be my last.

May I remember, remember, remember, not to forget, forget, forget.

Feel free to add to this list, but please notice there is a significant difference between this type of clarification and a host of popular affirmations that tend toward the superficial—all the "I am special" and "Share my gifts" kinds of stuff that are ego-boosting rather than soul-nourishing. You don't need to boost yourself; life will do that if you but remind yourself of who you are and what a good human life is about. Such simple reminders each day can make a major difference in the way our minds function.

REVIEWING AND REDEDICATING
YOURSELF FOR TOMORROW

If clarifying your motivation each morning is the front door, then looking back at the end of the day is the back door. Either at the end of your evening meditation period or when you're lying in bed before drifting off to sleep, take a few minutes to look back really honestly at the day you've just lived. His Holiness the Dalai Lama describes it this way:

> In the late evening, look back on the day to see if you really spent your day as you pledged in the morning. If you find something positive (beneficial, helpful), then good, feel happy! Reinforce that determination by rejoicing in your own good actions and by resolving to continue such activities in the future.
>
> If you find you have done something negative (harmful, destructive) during the day, you should feel remorse for those wrong actions committed . . . reflecting on how these same negative actions, committed in the past, are the reason why you are still experiencing undesirable consequences. Think

that if you continue to indulge in such activities in the future, this will lead you into similar undesirable consequences again.

This last step is important, because now with compassion for yourself, you can rededicate your commitment for tomorrow so that you don't have to feel bad tomorrow night as well. Be honest but gentle, firm but forgiving. *I'm humbled by today; may I be more consistent tomorrow for my own happiness and the happiness of all beings.*

LITTLE CLARIFICATIONS

In the Tibetan Buddhist tradition, motivation is extremely important. Clarifying your motivation can be useful even for the smallest issues of daily life. A well-loved monk in Tibet named Geshe Ben was especially known for his scrupulous self-honesty and holding himself to task for impure motivation. At a dinner for monks, Geshe Ben watched as the server moved down the table filling each monk's bowl with delicious-looking sweet curds. When the server finally arrived at his bowl, Geshe Ben put his hand over it and said, "I cannot have any, thank you. I have enjoyed much more than my share already!"

As you reach for something to eat, ask yourself, "What is my motivation? Am I hungry or bored or looking for a particular taste in my mouth?" As you turn on the television, ask yourself "Am I hoping to see something of value or just to be distracted?" In conversation, occasionally inquire of yourself, "What's the purpose of saying what I'm about to say? Is it to share, to inspire, to help, to give, to learn—or just to compete for attention, impress others, put my two cents in?"

This process of clarifying motivation should not be confused with psychologically analyzing ourselves to death. When clarifying, we are looking for a here-and-now realization of what is actually going on. We are applying our powers of observation, not our intellect. Clarifying motivation takes a moment or two. It is not concerned with *why* we may be using food or television as a distraction, just that we are; and it reminds us that we do not wish to continue such habit patterns.

As simple as it sounds, this is a solid beginning for living a happier, holier life. We can change enormously. We can become happy, peaceful people no matter what we've been through, or what we feel like right now. And we can begin very simply by clarifying our reasons for doing what we do, from big to little, every day. Like Michelangelo, every day we chip away a little more of whatever obscures the radiant inner self. Ah, the joy . . .

Spirituality Is Not Optional

What if I want a happy and meaningful life but I'm not particularly religious? What if I don't believe there is such a thing as God and even consider myself an atheist?

It is said that a king wearing full battle armor once rushed up to see the Buddha. The king said, "O Enlightened One, I am on my way to war and it is very possible I may be killed. So I am in need of your deepest spiritual teachings. However, I must hurry or my soldiers will lose their courage. Can you sum up all your teachings in one word?" The Buddha replied, "Awareness."

Not religion. Not God. Not faith. Just awareness.

There is an enormous difference between the choice to practice a religion and the need to become more spiritually aware. Religion is created by man. But life itself—creation, the universe, whatever we want to call it—*is* spiritual. That's not an opinion or a philosophy or a view. Transcendent experiences are not merely relative; it is not as though they are real if you believe in them and not real if you don't. The Divine is not an idea or a metaphor. It is a direct perception when we reach pure awareness.

*Ever is He present with you—think not He is
     far:
By the Master's teaching, recognize Him within
     yourself.*

—Adi Granth

We can move through life stubbornly insisting that we don't believe in a heart or lungs, but our life itself is supported by a heart and lungs that function in the background despite our foolishness. Any sensible person would smile at someone who contended there is no such thing as a heart. A sage who is experiencing Divine Nature smiles similarly at the eloquent conclusions of an atheist who insists there is no Divine Nature. Reality is not up for grabs.

Theism need not suggest a bearded, chauvinistic, wrathful God in order to impart that there is indeed intelligence, wonder, and sublime goodness inherent in creation. Life is designed intricately, and there are rules and laws that apply to us all. We can hold our breath till we turn blue, but we will not succeed in getting any sage to say that life is unspiritual. Life *is* spiritual. If we wish to be in tune with the order of the universe, we need to develop our spiritual awareness. If we do not develop any spiritual awareness, we will not be in tune. These are facts, not suggestions.

Followers of various faiths may contend that the single word the Buddha conveyed to the king should have been "love," or "obedience," or "devotion," or "faith." But all those other qualities will arise naturally and effortlessly when proper awareness has been attained. After all, the Old Testament itself does not say, "Be loving and know that I am God," or "Be obedient and know that I am God." The Old Testament says, "Be *still* and know that I am God."

When we become profoundly still, and merely see things

as they truly are, everything else falls into place. As you have probably experienced in your own life, without proper awareness love can easily become neediness, obedience can become oppression, devotion can become obsession, and faith can become superstition. So we begin by developing clearer and more honest awareness. The safest, most universal way of doing that is to practice one form or another of meditation.

Meditation practice is not about doing anything, religious or otherwise; it is about the long, patient struggle to stop doing everything. It is not about thinking holy thoughts; it is about gradually freeing the mind from all thoughts so that we may experience what Jung would have called the Universal Mind.

The idea of moving beyond ourselves—leaving behind all our personal judgments, biases, and scores to settle with life—is not appealing to everybody. In the sixties, I was one of many atheistic radicals who viewed meditation as a self-indulgent cop-out, a counterrevolutionary act. But when Sita and I finally tried it, and became diligent meditators in the early seventies, we realized that meditation may in fact be the most revolutionary act a human being can perform. Why? Because it leads us to see reality and acknowledge it with bare honesty. Which means ultimately, as the great teacher Krishnamurti put it, we stop relying so much on external authority. We see the truth of our nature, and therefore the truth of all human nature, and we have the opportunity to follow that truth regardless of cultural fads or fashions or fears. That's very revolutionary.

The first meditation course Sita and I took introduced us to an Eastern spiritual bent. We started practicing meditation every day, and soon began to open the Bible and other spiritual books such as the *Gospel of Ramakrishna, Be*

Here Now, and the *Tao Te Ching.* Whether Judeo-Christian-Islamic or Hindu-Buddhist, Eastern or Western or Native, the teachings seemed to speak to our very own yearnings, our spoken and unspoken hopes and dreams throughout years of seeking a deeper view of life than what we could see around us in the mainstream culture. It amazed us that such answers and guidance had been right under our noses all along. The practice of daily meditation was bringing the life of the world's great spiritual traditions into our hearts, rather than merely their ideas into our minds.

We practiced meditation with Buddhists, chanted with Hindus, prayed in churches, synagogues, and mosques, developed genuine awe of nature with Native Americans, and learned a wealth of sacred stories from all over the world. We found ourselves comfortable worshiping the one living Divine Essence with people of virtually any church or faith, because the underlying similarities of all the great traditions seemed far stronger to us than any differences between them. All the traditions seemed to be saying, "Become aware of the Loving Truth and then live accordingly." It kept getting back to our own awareness. How can anyone be atheistic about that?

As the Buddha summed up to the king, independent of how many teachers or sages we meet or how many churches or retreats we attend, the final proof of spiritual life is our moment-by-moment awareness. The degree to which we are able to see honestly who we are, what we need to do, and how we relate to the world is the degree to which our minds are noisy or quiet. Meditation practice is the classic universal technique for seeing life more honestly, with a quiet and undistracted mind. This sort of awareness brings more power for our lives into our own hands and hearts. By "quiet and undistracted mind," I simply mean a mind open to the present moment of reality, without the intrusion of all sorts of memories, symbols, behavior patterns, likes and dislikes, opinions, assumptions—all of the ego's encumbrances that pull us to interpret life in biased or limited ways. That's the kind of quieting meditation helps us do.

Zen Buddhism, one tradition that focuses almost exclusively on meditation practice, uses the term *Shunyata* (emptiness). By cultivating an "empty" mind, the idea is not to be like a zombie or devoid of life's qualities. It is actually the opposite: emptiness of mind refers to being fully present in the wonder and magnificence of existence.

Father Bede Griffith, a well-known Benedictine monk who spent many years in India as part of the interfaith dialogue, put it this way in an ecstatic exclamation: "I dissolved into the emptiness, and discovered it was *filled* with Love!" Shunyata meets Agape. The beautiful reconciliation between East and West. This is the realm of meditative awareness.

I do admit that until we experience our own direct awareness of life's innate spirituality, we are advised to have faith in something—an idea, a teacher, a saint, a religion, a prayer, a sacred text, a body of practices. Something we consider beautiful, noble; something to help us move forward toward spiritual realities we have not yet experienced ourselves. We take a path, on faith, into our everyday lives, into our strengths and weaknesses and hopes and fears and disappointments, and endeavor to walk it.

But this need not be blind faith. This is not a game of pin-the-tail-on-the-donkey. With eyes wide open, we can read scriptures or texts of various traditions, meet elders of those traditions, read biographies of the holy men and holy women who followed a certain path, visit communities organized around certain teachings. We can visit a worship service, try some of the practices ourselves, and feel intuitively whether something clicks deep within us. If we took the same amount of time and energy to look into various faith paths that we spend on selecting a new car (and then paying for it!), we'd have a wealth of information to draw upon.

But mainly we can immediately begin to practice meditation. Meditation is the cornerstone practice for developing spiritual awareness. It has been a part of every great tradition. As our meditative awareness expands, our props and questions and doubts can fall away, just like the scaffolding falls away when a rocket is launched. We see for ourselves, usually accompanied by great joy and relief, that we are not who we thought we were. When a devotee asked the great master Ramana Maharshi, "Will meditation answer all my questions?" the master smiled and answered, "No, but it will destroy the questioner." We need not take on anyone else's beliefs forever. All we need is to become truly aware.

A Practice: CLASSIC BREATH-CENTERED MEDITATION

Meditation is not easy. We have spent a lifetime allowing the mind to be uncontrolled, so it is no minor task to begin reining it in. The mind does not like to consider itself as merely one facet of our identity. Our sense of self is all wrapped up in our thoughts and feelings. Meditation practice brings us to experience mind as mind, emotions as emotions, and self as self.

This is a threat to the mind's turf, so we encounter numerous forms of resistance when we begin to practice.

One friend of mine experienced tremendous shoulder pain only when he sat down to meditate. He eventually took it as a message to give up meditation. If your resolve is that shaky, you will definitely find compelling reasons to give up the practice. If, instead, your shoulders (or knees, back, neck, etc.) get the idea that you are definitely going to continue meditating one way or another, then your body will begin to adapt itself to be more comfortable to your new discipline.

TAKING A VOW

The best way to give meditation a fair chance is to take a vow to complete at least one month of regular practice at the same time each day. Twenty to thirty minutes is usually recommended, but even ten or fifteen minutes will give you a good idea of whether it affects your life. Decide everything in advance: exactly how long your daily sittings will be, where and at what time, what you will sit on (see below), how you will time your practice.

By preparing in this way, you will be giving your ego's resistance the least possible leverage. Resistance is often expressed by constant "improvements" over the original plans. Don't fall for that. You can change things at the end of the month. Keep your vow even if you get sick or have a bad night's sleep.

Try not to create excuses for looking around or moving about. For example, set your watch or a timer for however long you wish to sit, and then do not allow yourself to check on the time during your practice. Also, choose a regular time for your practice, one that is not likely to be interrupted; make arrangements in advance to be free from phone calls or knocks on the door. No matter how sweet your dog or cat may be, don't attempt to meditate with a pet on your lap or close enough to lick or nuzzle your feet. Give the practice your formal respect.

Meditation practice is not like flipping on a light switch. It is more like turning up a dimmer switch in tiny, unnoticeable increments. So give yourself the freedom of not evaluating day by day whether it's "working" or whether you enjoy it or not. Commit to a month or two months or even three, and just practice faithfully for that whole period before you look back and determine whether it seems valuable to you.

HOW TO SIT

It is well worth your time to pay attention to the actual physical part of sitting to meditate. On the one hand, nobody gets spiritual brownie points for looking like a great yogi or enduring unnecessary pain in the knees and back. On the other hand, you won't gain much control over your mind if you slump over into a half sleep every time you try to meditate, or if you shift constantly trying to find a good position. Lying down to meditate is generally not a good idea, inasmuch as it is deeply associated with sleep.

What's important is a sitting posture that keeps the back, neck, and head in a straight line yet is so balanced that you can hold yourself in place with no tension. For most of us this takes some practice. Try sitting on pillows or folded blankets, and see what height allows you to sit straight with no effort. The knees should be down, not up, when your bottom is at the right height. When the knees are down, the back is naturally straight.

Another sitting position is called *seiza* in Japanese. You sit slightly higher, straddling the pillows like a saddle, with your feet behind you. This is very comfortable for many people who can't sit cross-legged. Just be sure to get up high enough that your feet don't fall asleep and your knees don't ache. Sitting in a chair is also all right, although a tendency is to lean against the back of the chair, and that usually isn't very straight. If you do sit in a chair, don't lean; also make sure your feet and legs are symmetrical: cross your legs at the ankles or place both feet flat on the floor a few inches apart.

In all of these sitting postures, the hands should be placed either on each leg or in the lap so that their weight does not pull down the shoulders. Hands can be loosely clasped or held separate. Traditionally, they're kept closed to some degree, since an open hand is a gesture of going outward, and meditation is a time to go inward.

FOCUSING ON THE BREATH

One of the most universal meditation methods is to use your own breath as the focus of your concentration.

1. After getting the body straight and still, bring all your attention to one of these two points: the tip of your nose, where the breath automatically goes in and out, or the lower abdomen, where the diaphragm rises with each in-breath and falls with each out-breath.

Whether you choose the nose or the diaphragm, keep the mind right there, feeling the whole movement of each breath in and out. Don't follow it in or out; just keep the attention in one spot, observing how it feels as it goes by.

The breath is a very good focus for concentration. Because it's fresh every second, it helps bring the mind into the present moment. And the present moment is the only place in which true meditation ever happens (in fact, it's the only place *anything* ever really happens).

2. Time and time again—maybe hundreds of times in a half hour—your mind will wander, and you'll forget all about observing your breath. But the instant you remember that you forgot, simply drop the chain of thoughts in midstream and get right back to the nose or the diaphragm. There's no sense being frustrated by distractions, because frustration is just another distraction. Remember, this isn't really meditation, anyway; it's meditation practice. If we were already good at it, we wouldn't need to practice.

3. When using the breath as a meditation method, you do not need to breathe in any special way or to try to control the breathing at all. The idea is to observe the breath however it is. Sometimes it may be long and slow, other times short and fast; no matter. You may notice that the breath may change as your thoughts change. Anxious or fearful thoughts tend to quicken the breath; peaceful thoughts tend to slow it down. This is part of the self-education process. No need to do anything but observe and learn.

4. It may be helpful to channel your mind by thinking "Breathing in . . ." as you feel the breath go in, and "Breathing out . . ." as you feel the breath go out. But try to make sure that you feel the breath the entire time; don't get stuck in the thought.

5. If your mind seems particularly wild sometimes, it may help to do the following focusing exercise until it comes back under control. As you feel the breath come in, think "Breathing in," and then count the breath as it goes out: "Breathing in . . . , one; breathing in . . . , two; breathing in . . . , three," and so forth up to ten, then start at one again. The only rule is, if you lose track of what number you're on—even if you're only slightly unsure—start over.

You may be amazed that sometimes your mind is so scattered that you can lose count between one and two! It's happened to me many times. This exercise can be a good occasional indicator of how well or poorly your concentration is coming along.

6. The very last moments of a meditation practice should always be to reconnect with the world in a productive way. For example, centering your attention in your heart, you can extend blessings of goodwill outward in all directions. You can do this visually, seeing in your mind's eye a wave of light, or concentric circles of light, emanating from you and enveloping the world, so that no one is unloved or uncared for at that moment.

Or you may do this more verbally than visually, silently expressing prayers like "May all beings find their way," or spontaneous thoughts of compassion toward individuals or the whole world. In one way or another, it is important to end meditation periods by extending ourselves outward. This helps us remember that we are not meditating merely to enjoy ourselves or to benefit ourselves in isolation from all other beings.

Basic breath-centered meditation is a simple but powerful technique you can work with on your own. However, if you have the time and inclination, attending a meditation retreat would be a big step forward. And occasionally it can be helpful to do a guided meditation in addition to your ongoing daily practice. There are countless forms of guided meditation. I include one below to give you an idea.

MOUNTAIN AND WIND MEDITATION

There are two questions about meditation that I hear quite often. One is, "How do I get my mind quiet?" The other is, "What do I do about all the noise around me?"

While a quiet mind may sometimes be the result of spiritual practice, it's impossible to *make* the mind quiet. Our heart's nature is to process blood, our lungs' to process air, and our mind's to process thoughts. Too much focus on trying to push thoughts away or "go blank" will distract us from developing our meditation practice.

With that in mind, here is a guided meditation that may help you put the noise in your mind—as well as external noise—into a perspective that will enable you to keep up your effort without going nuts while the mind rebels. It is my own adaptation of a simple form of Vipassana, or insight, meditation from the Theravadin Buddhist tradition, which I developed for prisoners and others who deal with high levels of internal and external noise.

1. Place your body in a comfortable meditation posture (as described above). Get really stable, and then pay full attention to how solid and still you feel. Feel the body as if it were an immovable mountain. The body is indeed like a mountain to the billions of organisms on it and inside it. Feel this immensity. Feel the countless life forms and activities you are hosting with no effort on your part, just as a real mountain shelters herds of various animals, waterfalls, rivers, and so on, yet does nothing at all. Strengthen this sense of hugeness and stability for a few minutes.
2. Begin to feel the movement of the breath, like the steady breeze blowing across the mountain. It is the mountain's

nature not to move, while it is the wind's nature never to stop moving. Same thing with body and breath, both follow their nature.

3. If outside noise begins to intrude on your practice, or when the mind kicks in with busy thoughts, old songs, analyses, and so on, merely experience these intrusions as a radio that someone left playing in a meadow somewhere on the mountainside. It blares whatever it may be blaring, but it has no effect on the stability of the mountain or the ceaseless flowing of the wind. The mountain doesn't identify with the radio. It doesn't try to ignore the radio, it just lets it play, remaining undisturbed by the noise. Body sitting, breath flowing, mind playing in the background—all perfect, all peaceful, all following their nature.

4. Stay this way for ten to twenty minutes. Do not be frustrated by how many times you get lost in a stream of thought; just patiently recover your practice as soon as you "remember you forgot," as the Russian mystic Gurdjieff put it. Be patient as well as persistent.

5. Toward the end of your sitting, let the breath flow a little more deeply, but slowly, and recognize how good it feels to experience your "mountain-ness" and "wind-ness." Nothing to do or stop doing, feeling very strong and solid. Notice it. Enjoy it. Let the mountain smile almost imperceptibly. Make a mental note to remember this state the next time you feel small or powerless. Also remember this state the next time you see a mountain in the wind.

Meditation is not easy. The mind can be pretty wild, stubborn, and chaotic. But if you stick with meditation, gradually, like a ship in stormy seas with a deep anchor, your mind will stop tossing about so much. As the storm settles, and our minds come to accept the idea that we practice regular meditation, we will probably feel better and do better in virtually every area of our lives. Meditation practice enhances physical health, strengthens our concentration and acumen for learning just about anything, increases our patience and equanimity, and helps mightily with impulse control, such as handling anger. This is all the result of increased awareness, nothing more—the single word of advice the Buddha imparted to the warrior king.

You Can Do Hard

—————— 🍃 ——————

So many times in my life I've tried to start living better by exercising or meditating regularly, or cutting back on how much I drink. I can never keep it up, even though I feel better when I do these things. Why is it so hard to change habits? How can I be more effective in making changes?

Changing for the better is one of the most fundamental human urges, yet most of us are more sophisticated about how to use cell phones and VCRs than we are about how to change bad habits into good ones. We may go around and around in the same circles all our lives rather than consider that perhaps we're not seeing our behavior patterns clearly or that we're failing to respect the process of change itself.

This is not new territory. Two thousand years ago, Paul lamented:

> My own behavior baffles me. For I find myself not doing what I really want to do, but doing what I really loathe. . . . I often find that I have the will to do good, but not the power. That is, I don't accomplish the good I set out to do, and the evil I don't really want to do I find I am always doing. . . . What a wretched man I am!
>
> —Romans 7:15–24

Is there even one of us who has not shared Paul's frustration? Yet we know that change—even major, enormous change—is still possible. Let's not overlook the fact that, for all his self-proclaimed wretchedness, Paul went on to become a saint.

Changing for the better is not only within our reach, it is also among our prime responsibilities as members of the human community. It is downright sinful to give up on ourselves. The world needs us to become joyful and enlightened human beings. Like Paul, even after countless instances of "the evil I don't really want to do I find I am always doing," we must hang in there and keep trying.

Change can be grueling. But by being grueling, it unearths the very best in us—our latent courage, patience, humility, determination, empathy, compassion—so many essential qualities for our continuing spiritual journey. For example, by the time we go through the rigors of quitting a twenty-year smoking habit, we may be stronger, wiser, and more empathetic human beings. The *object* of change— quitting smoking—becomes almost trivial compared to what we can gain from the *process* of quitting. And the harder it is, the more we stand to gain.

We have a saying around Kindness House, the community where I live: "You can do hard." The reason we say this is that, in our modern era, the words "It's too hard" have become an anthem for giving up. Have an ache or pain, reach for a pill; get depressed after losing a job, take Prozac for a while. A friend once confided to me that she regretted divorcing her husband. She said the only reason she did it was a prevailing attitude at the time that "If it gets really hard, why make yourself suffer?" Maybe we have become afraid to tackle anything that might be very hard; maybe we've been convinced that we can't do hard things.

"You can do hard" is one of my community's ways of reminding us that we need not run away in fear just because
something is greatly challenging. It might be daunting, but
we can do daunting. It might even be scary, but we can do
scary. No matter how bad it is—and it could be very bad
for a while—we can do it. And then, years later, it's just one
sentence: "Sita and I hated each other for most of 1979; we
held on to our marriage by a thread." Just one little sentence in a conversation. Nothing extraordinary. Nobody
falls over when you tell them.

We can do hard. Really, we can. Don't let a brief cultural
myopia fool you into thinking you'll crumble when the
chips are down. Human beings were designed for the chips
to be down sometimes. We can endure some unimaginably
hard things and come out better for them.

Sita and I have met people like the Dalai Lama's assistant
physician, who spent ten years being tortured in a Chinese
prison camp. He is a quiet, untraumatized, unbitter man
with great compassion and a healthy sense of humor. And,
of course, in our prison work we have met thousands of
people who endured many years of brutal conditions right
here in America, and who managed to deepen their wisdom and compassion rather than become brutal them
selves. We human beings can do hard.

This is the first step toward understanding the process of
real, lasting change: simply knowing with certainty that
you can do whatever you need to do. This understanding
has a dual edge: On the one hand it increases your confidence and dignity. On the other hand, it places full responsibility on you if you fail to make the change you set out to
make. But this is a good thing, not a guilt trip. If you set
out to quit smoking and you cave in halfway through the
process, you must accept that you are choosing not to make

the full effort at this time. When you feel up to it, you can choose to make the effort. Same with meditating every day or losing weight or anything else within reason. Accept that you have the power to change.

The second step toward understanding the process of change is to look very honestly at the change or changes you are trying to make, and decide whether they would serve your true self-improvement or only your vanity. For example, I have worked out with weights since I was fourteen years old. Being a bodybuilder actually saved my life when I had a big car wreck at age eighteen. I have a lot of affection and gratitude for lifting weights, and have always had some degree of vanity about being muscular.

Now that I'm in my fifties, it's a good idea for me to continue working out, but in a very different way than vanity may tempt. Vanity would like me to continue lifting heavy weights and looking chiseled. But for my overall health, for the prevention of injuries, and devotion to my primary service work, it is more appropriate for me to leave the heavy weights and chiseled bodies to the younger generation. Now I do a light dumbbell workout for about a half hour, just three days a week. My younger persona can't believe I've "caved in" like this! Self-discipline can sometimes take an ironic form.

Besides vanity, there are other motivations for change or discipline that are not in our best interests. They usually come under the heading "fighting nature," and that may be the reason we fail time and time again. The jogger who is bound and determined not to allow age to affect his regimen, the perpetual dieter who insists on getting back to the weight she was when she was twenty-five—such people are fighting nature. The media glorify these attitudes as "the fighting spirit," but aging is not an enemy. There's nothing wrong with having a little middle-age spread or needing more rest. If I tried to keep my waist a size 30, as it measured most of my life, I would be in a constant state of tension, whereas keeping a size 32 is virtually effortless because it's more natural. If I tried to keep the same pace in my lecture tours now that I kept ten or twenty years ago, I would run myself into the ground. I certainly keep a good diet and stay fit, but I don't want to waste my energy trying to impede or deny the aging process.

I encourage you to examine the changes you wish to make in your life and be honest with yourself about your motivation. That way, when you do choose to make a change, you will feel undivided about it and therefore more committed to whatever effort may be required of you.

The third step is to remember the importance of the process itself. All the effort we spend in self-discipline, all the difficulties we face in changing habitual behavior or facing deep-seated fears, are neither wasted nor incidental. They are potent spiritual curricula for our lifelong benefit. The qualities we discover in ourselves will come in handy countless times throughout our lives. Understanding this may help us to be good sports at the times we feel overwhelmed by the effort required of us. It places our adventure of change on a higher and broader playing field.

Imagine a runner who begins a race and, after running twenty yards, has to jump over a hurdle. *Damn it, what's this thing doing here? It's in my way!* Another twenty yards, another hurdle. *Damn!* Then another, and another. As his annoyance grows, he loses focus, risks injury, loses steam.

But knowing from the outset that the race is actually a hurdle event puts everything in a completely different perspective, doesn't it? The same effort may be required, the same hurdles may need to be jumped, but now they are part of the fun instead of being unwelcome obstacles. Bad habits, and qualities or situations that need to be changed, are hurdles in our lives, not obstacles. We waste enormous power if we misunderstand this.

A fourth step in the process of successful change is to make sure we do not expect any one particular change to make our lives perfect from that moment on. That's a sure setup for a letdown. Life continues to present hurdles. It is futile to make changes in order to extort a hurdle-free life from God. We make the change, God doesn't deliver as we had presumed, and then we say the hell with it and revert to our old patterns.

The old saying "Virtue is its own reward" is significant here. Change is its own reward and has many hidden rewards, but it is not a tool of negotiation for extracting favors from life or from God. In my own experience, whenever we go eyeball to eyeball with life or with God, we lose. God never blinks first.

Change also does not get us closer to God. We don't make all these changes to get closer to God; there's no distance in the first place. We can't get any closer than we already are. We do spiritual work to become more aware and less distracted, so we can enjoy the depths of this perpetual closeness.

A yoga teacher I know was always fretting about the souls of his beer-guzzling, couch-potato friends who weren't living spiritually. But the beer-guzzling couch potatoes are just as close to God as you or I; what else could they be? As Krishna says in the Bhagavad Gita, "There is spirit alone in this universe. There is no second thing." Beer, television, couch potatoes, all spirit. No second thing. This is an important reality check for those of us who work hard on personal change. It is crucial that we don't get uppity about it.

Don't get me wrong; I'm not saying it doesn't matter what we do. Life is a miraculous and sacred event. Living a lazy life, avoiding challenges, satisfying only our crude whims and hungers—all this is like owning the original Mona Lisa painting and using it as a dartboard. That's crazy and wasteful, but it is still the Mona Lisa, whether we cherish it or not. And we are all still equally made of God, whether we reflect it in our life patterns or not.

There is so much power to this realization. It can lighten us up tremendously. We can stop judging ourselves and others so harshly. We can stop struggling as if we're always coming from behind. Best of all, we can let go of the false notion that our spiritual work is some sort of obligation on our part. Instead, we can see more clearly that changing for the better is a joy of the highest order.

Once we see this, our perspective changes completely. Instead of thinking in terms of starting "good" habits or breaking "bad" habits, we start to consider how each habit affects our lives. We begin to see how dulling our mind with alcohol or numbing our feelings through television, for example, simply gets in the way of being our true self. Change is no longer a vague or moralistic burden, or an insurmountable barrier.

When we see everything in a larger context, we become more willing and eager to sweep away anything that might prevent us from touching true joy. This last step might be summed up as understanding what change can and can't accomplish: It can help us enjoy life's richness; it cannot make life itself any richer. All the spirit, the fullness, the sacredness, is already here for the taking.

A Practice: VOW PRACTICE

Because change usually requires sustained commitment, one of the best ways to get that commitment rolling is to take a vow in the presence of others. Vow practice is more formal than making verbal resolutions. Most of us at Kindness House work regularly with vow practice, and we have found it extremely helpful for making real and lasting changes. The basic elements of the practice are *preparation, declaration,* and *implementation.*

1. *Preparation:* Plan ahead. Vows taken impulsively (especially when we are angry toward ourselves) usually don't last. Spend time in prayer and reflection about any changes you want to make—major or minor, lifelong or temporary. Think ahead to the ways your vow may affect your life, your friendships, your future plans, and so on, and accept those consequences. There is no gain without some amount of sacrifice or loss.

   Next, work on the wording of your vow. One prisoner friend wanted to take a vow of total silence for a year. I said, "What if a guard speaks to you and requires you to answer?" We advised him to do two things: include in the wording of his vow something like "except in cases of genuine emergency or having to respond to an official," and let the warden know about his desire to take a vow of silence and ask for his cooperation. Mature planning makes for a more feasible vow.

   The most important preparatory step for a vow is this: Don't take it until you know you will keep it. If you're unsure of whether you can live up to "I will always . . ." or

"I will never . . . ," then use the wording "I will *strive to* . . ." That way, your sworn commitment is to try, and sometimes this may actually work better anyway. If you do say "never" or "forever," that's fine, but understand the gravity of what you are pledging.

You may wish to make a time limit to the vow. If the idea of quitting smoking forever is too scary, make a vow not to smoke for one month or one week—even one day if that's all you think you can do. Throughout this book you will see short-term vows dealing with right speech, blaming others, watching television, and so on, which can be helpful for looking at specific problem areas. Vow practice can be very versatile.

Once spoken, you are bound. That's the central power of vows. Honoring promises is essential for self-respect and any success in life. So think carefully about your vows, discuss them with someone you trust, and write them down word for word (no shorthand or outline).

2. *Declaration:* Once a vow has been properly prepared, the next step is to "declare" it in a little ceremony with one or more friends as witnesses. This is important, because as in a marriage ceremony, you are obligating yourself publicly to follow your vow. If you break it, others will know you have let yourself down. You will have let them down as well, because they may not have as much faith in themselves after seeing you break your vow.

It is important to commit yourself in front of others, and it is also encouraging to know they support your struggle to abide by the promises you have made. After you declare your vow, the witness or other friends can say something like, "We respect your vow, and we receive your vow." In my own community, that's the step of declaration. We usually do this while bowing to each other with respect.

3. *Implementation:* Then comes the bottom line—day by day, abiding by the vow you have taken. I strongly encourage you to repeat your vow aloud, alone, at the beginning of every day. Read it or recite it as sincerely as you did that first day, and remember the feelings that prompted you to take your vow. That way, you are actually taking the vow every day.

Remember to respect all vows equally. Whether it is to stop eating sweets for a week or never to take a sip of alcohol for the rest of your life, a vow must be respected fully. A sincere vow is an expression of your willingness to work, to sacrifice, to change. It shows that you understand how life works—that change doesn't come just because you whine about it. Real, lasting change requires planning, effort, and perseverance.

A vow is also a great way to initiate yourself into daily spiritual practices. Vow to do any of the practices in this book at the same time each day for one month. Then, whether you are sick or well, tired or alert, bored or restless, you just do it. It doesn't matter whether you feel like it, or whether it seems to be doing you any good, or whether you're good at it; you've taken a vow to do it anyway. What a relief! By giving up some minor freedoms of changing your mind, you give yourself major freedom to change your life. Try it and see.

It's Not the Top, It's the Climb

I think I want to try a spiritual practice, but they all seem to require a lot of time and effort. How do I know I'll get what I want from it? I don't want to waste my time.

From time to time, students of budo [martial arts] wonder if the large amount of time they are putting into their practice is worth what they are "getting out of it." While this seems to be a reasonable question, it actually reveals a fundamental lack of understanding. The time that one puts into the practice of an art *is* what one is getting out of it. It is the process of training that is truly valuable, not some eventual goal. All of life truly exists only at this instant.

—H. E. Davey, *Unlocking the Secrets of Aiki-Jujitsu*

In the mid-1980s, when my son, Josh, was fourteen, I was asked to accompany a small group of kids from his school on an Outward Bound wilderness training course. I had heard a lot of good things about those courses, so I jumped at the opportunity to experience one. Off we went to the mountains of North Carolina for five days of ropes courses, rock climbing, rappelling down cliffs, and backpacking. I've always seen that Outward Bound experience as a good reflection of the spiritual journey, and an excellent teaching about "right view."

For one thing, the events themselves—the considerable physical challenges—demand all of your attention during the course. But they're virtually meaningless except as a way in which to develop your inner qualities. It's the same way in our lives—the daily, practical world may require most of our attention, but it would be crazy to forget the spiritual purpose behind every situation we face.

Picture signing up for the Outward Bound course, then spending the whole time just trying to get out of the damn woods—not learning how to keep dry in the rain or use a compass, not noticing the many opportunities to build courage and let go of fear.

In contrast, if I were to say, "I must develop courage," and then sit in a chair to think about courage, that's not going to accomplish much either. The ropes course—climbing a skinny rope ladder forty feet up a tree, then walking across a narrow, slippery log during a light drizzle, and then grabbing onto another rope to swing all the way down to the ground—gave me a tangible opportunity to look at fear and courage.

There's nothing very important or noble about climbing a tree or swinging down a rope. How does that help the world? Yet courage definitely helps the world, and it can't be seen, heard, or felt by itself. It's like trying to see a color; color is real, yet we can never see it by itself. We can see red paint, black pen, blue sky, but we can never see pure redness, blackness, or blueness by themselves?

According to the sages, our lives are solely a journey into

our Divine Nature—love, Godliness, holiness, however you want to say it. That's the important part, like courage at the ropes course. The ropes are merely the vehicle for the development of courage. Life is merely the vehicle for the awakening of our souls. Every person and situation in our lives is merely an "inward bound" ropes course or boulder or cliff, designed precisely to bring out the best or worst in us so that we can eventually come home into our Divine Nature. So, what's the point of signing up for the course and then complaining that the events are too hard?

In the rock-climbing event at Outward Bound, we were asked to climb a very sheer boulder about thirty feet high. I remember looking at the top of the boulder while I was on the ground waiting for my turn. The people who had made the climb were standing around the top, looking incredibly happy and radiant and exhilarated. What an easy (and common) mistake it would have been to think, "Wow, they look so happy; there must be something really great at the top of that boulder!" Of course, there was nothing spectacular at the top of the boulder. Those people were enjoying the rewards of a tough climb. But how many times in our lives do we forget that, and merely try to get to the top of each boulder by every other means except going through the same effort and risks the people at the top went through?

I caught myself thinking that way awhile back, in a conversation with one of my favorite spiritual elders, Father Murray Rogers, an Anglican priest who lived in India, Israel, and China for many years. I had just returned from India, and we were talking about my meeting with His Holiness the Dalai Lama of Tibet. I said that His Holiness was probably the most profoundly simple, deeply happy person I have ever met. Father Murray's response was, "Yes, and just imagine the pain and struggle he must have endured in order to become so thoroughly happy." I was seeing the Dalai Lama at the top of the boulder, and Father Murray's response reminded me that it was the climb that made him who he is. What we see in saints is the result of a long, hard climb, not a lucky break or an avoidance of difficulty.

You and I have every opportunity to make that same climb. And, of course, we're doing it all the time, whether we like it or not. It's just that we can climb with ignorance, fear, avoidance, denial, complaints, whining, and so forth, or with excitement, gratitude, respectfulness, perseverance, and rock-solid faith.

The purpose of spiritual practice is not to get to the top with less effort; we will each be called upon to expend tremendous effort—to forgive the unforgivable, bear the unbearable, surmount the insurmountable. We will be called upon to move beyond personal prejudices and jealousies, neediness and phobias, the fear of aging and dying, the loss of everyone we love. There is no easy, painless way through life.

The purpose of personal spiritual practice is to maintain our overview, our awareness that our struggles, our boulders, are never random or purposeless: the top is nothing except for the proper climb up to it. If yours seems to be a very tough climb, you may find even more joy at the top. People who have no overview, who find no value in the rigors of the climb, are bound to be sorely disappointed when they reach the top. The best help we can offer is to recognize that we are all climbers, and to make sure we are willing to lend a positive spirit about the climb, as well as a hand, when called upon.

For example, we may one day find the boulder of cancer staring us, or a loved one, in the face. At the top of that boulder is either survival or death. As many of us have seen in our own lives or in the lives of others, it can be of tremendous value not to forget the preciousness and transformative potential of that climb—the handholds we grab, the decisions we make, the attitudes we cultivate, the relationships we heal. Those who make the most of the climb seem to be joyous at the top whether they find life or death there. Those to whom the climb is a fearful, reluctant ordeal do not seem to get much out of the top one way or another. That's what happens when we lose our view that life is actually more about the climb than about the top.

If we really begin to work with the point this chapter makes, then we must look at the possibility that perhaps some of our fears are with us for the purpose of overcoming them. We need not take this to silly extremes, such as becoming a daredevil who leaps thirty schoolbuses on a motorcycle. Fear of injury and death actually has a role to play in keeping us in one piece.

But many of our fears do not seem so instinctive or reasonable. For many years, Sita had a phobic fear of being upside down. It was so strong that she wondered whether she may have been killed that way in another lifetime or something along those lines. Whatever the original source, however, her fear did not seem to serve a good purpose in *this* life. It prevented her from doing shoulder stands or headstands in yoga, it caused anxiety when she dove into a pool or encountered a wave in the ocean. More than anything else, it was simply a heavy stone in her backpack of life, and she grew tired of lugging it around.

One day in 1981, Sita asked me and another friend to help her surmount this lifelong fear (she was thirty-seven at the time). We spent the next seven hours in an exhausting and grueling contest between her fear and her determination. What she had asked us to do was simply to help her stand on her head by lifting her legs. We were not to take the battle away from her by forcing her legs up, but rather just to give her moral support and simple balance.

That may sound undemanding, but anyone who has ever dealt with a phobia may readily understand how much screaming and resistance took place during our hundreds of attempts to help her get her legs fully over her head. We had to shut all the windows so the neighbors wouldn't think a murder was taking place.

Sita finally stood on her head, and then stood on her head again. And again. By the end of the day, she looked as exhilarated as the Outward Bound climbers on top of the boulder. For several weeks, I helped her stand on her head to make sure the phobic pattern could not find a way to slide back in place. Her backpack is one stone lighter now, and her step is therefore brighter and freer. She is no longer even curious about where the fear came from. It is gone.

A Practice: FACING FEARS

What stones do you carry in your pack that serve no purpose other than to weigh you down and slow your step? Are you afraid of the dark? Then find a safe place and an appropriate time to be alone in pitch blackness for a whole night. Are you terrified of snakes? Find an opportunity to spend some time in the presence of a nonpoisonous snake. Ideally, find a situation where you can actually handle the snake and take your time to relax around it. Are you loath to raise your hand and make a comment at a meeting or lecture? (At one time, public speaking was said to be the number one fear among Americans.) Then take a vow to do exactly that at the next opportunity. Confirm your vow silently at the beginning of the meeting, and be sure to fulfill it, even if you have nothing more to say than a few words of appreciation for the speaker or the meeting itself.

Sita's fear was phobic, but many of our fears are not so intense—they are more like a lot of pebbles in our pack, each one of which we can probably accommodate for a whole lifetime. But get the pebbles too. Each time we face and surmount a fear, we strengthen a host of qualities that are helpful in our spiritual journey.

And during the course of this journey to full God-realization, we will encounter a lot scarier things within ourselves than bugs or snakes or public speaking. Facing worldly fears is like basic training for facing more advanced fears in the depths of our practices.

Here are three general tips about this process of facing fears:

1. Breathe. In every way possible, begin training yourself now to reflexively turn to your breath during times of fear, stress, or confusion. The breath is a key component of all spiritual traditions. When you're afraid, stay with the breath and keep it flowing steadily and calmly. Breathe determination and confidence in with the in-breath, and fear out with the out-breath.

2. Whenever feasible, let at least one friend know what you are doing so that he or she understands and supports your intention. Even if you do not need a friend for tangible assistance, it can be very helpful to have someone bear witness to what you are doing. If the fear you are facing requires

being alone, the friend can still bear witness by knowing what you intend to do and when, and then offering you blessings from afar at that time, as well as helping you talk about it afterward.

3. As Sita did, make sure that the fear does not sneak back into your pack when you're not looking. You can decide the best way to do this based on the particular fear you choose to face.

Facing fears is like getting cavities filled: that day may be a drag, but we can feel the positive effects for years to come. Our self-respect, especially, moves up several notches when we see that we really mean it about becoming freer and less limited.

The Coal Miner's Faith

If only I knew what each day was going to bring, it would make life so much easier. How do I deal with the day-to-day craziness of my life, the kinds of unexpected crises and stressful incidents that come up as a matter of course in anyone's life? How do I keep my equilibrium and stay focused on what's really important?

A monk of the ancient Carthusian sect of Christianity once said, "The darkness of the future is the necessary space for the exercise of our liberty and our faith." I recommend spending a few moments to fully digest the phrase "necessary space for the exercise of our liberty and faith." In other words, if somehow we were able to know what each day was going to bring, there would be no need for free will or faith; indeed, no reason for the world to exist at all, since the primary purpose of life is to exercise free will and faith in such a way that we reach communion with God. The darkness of the future, the fact that we do not know what is to come, is crucial, not unfortunate.

Every spiritual tradition maintains that we are not victims of random crises or chaotic events; we share power and responsibility with God for the state of our lives and of the world. What is known in the East as the law of *karma* (Sanskrit for "action") is not only an Eastern idea. The Old Testament begins with God giving free will to Adam and Eve so that they can create their own karma, by obeying or disobeying his injunctions. Human karma in the Western traditions was set in motion the moment Adam and Eve chose to taste of the fruit of the tree of knowledge of good and evil. Ever since, the guiding principle has been "As ye sow, so shall ye reap."

If we knew the future, what would happen to our motivation for striving mightily to create a better life? What would happen to dedication and perseverance? Why would we bother facing a challenge? You might say, "Well, I don't mean that I want to know the entire future; it would just be nice to have a better idea of what tomorrow will bring." But each day to come builds the entire future. It is important that it be unknown to us so that we may be fully engaged in doing our best.

When we change our view to embrace this "darkness of the future" as a good thing, then we can stop dreading each day's surprises and stresses, and meet them instead with what could be called our cosmic sense of humor or profoundest level of good sportsmanship. Then we are not constantly thrown for a loop when the day does not go as planned. We never expected it to. As the renowned *New Yorker* cartoonist Gahan Wilson once remarked, "Life essentially doesn't work. So it's the basis of endless humor." That's the cosmic sense of humor I'm talking about.

Another example of that humor took place at a conference in Switzerland in the early 1990s. A woman asked all the panelists, "How do you see the world fifty years from now?" They all answered ponderously from their own areas of expertise, except for His Holiness the Dalai Lama of Tibet. He spoke last, and said, "Madam, I don't even know what kind of tea I'll be having with dinner tonight. How could I possibly know what will happen fifty years from now?" And then he laughed and laughed, as he does throughout the day.

There is great peace and happiness in the absence of pointless anxiety and in the acceptance of our proper sphere of concern—doing our very best, shining our very brightest, in this one little spot we find ourselves in. That's what we are designed to do. When we choose this acceptance, or faith, it doesn't mean that bad things no longer happen to us; it just means that there is no longer a tendency toward fear or bitterness in our pain. Fear implies we're unprotected, and bitterness implies something shouldn't have happened the way it did. Both are false to the person of faith.

Fear says, "You'd better watch out! It's dark up ahead!" But in the daily practice of faith, you can remind yourself, "Of course it's dark up ahead! Up ahead is not my business; this moment is, and it's light enough for me to see right now." A person of faith is like a coal miner carrying his light on his cap. Wherever he arrives, it's light enough for him to see. He doesn't look ahead and say, "But it's dark up there!" He knows that by the time he gets there, it will be at least dimly lit. If the whole mine were lit, the coal miner would have no use for his own light.

Our coal miner's light—our wisdom and intuition—comes from inside us. So it makes sense to work on brightening that light and keeping the batteries strong rather than worrying about what's in the dark up ahead. This is essentially what spiritual practices and a wholesome lifestyle are for—not to exempt us from life's ups and downs, but rather to help us maintain the sort of presence and awareness that can extract gold from what may seem at first glance to be worthless rock.

A Practice:
"ANYTHING THAT CAN HAPPEN" MANTRA

Are you willing to live fully with the darkness of the future? Are you willing to deal with the truth of life? This may sound like a stupid or trite question, but I discovered a lot about myself by grappling with its ramifications. In the early nineties I spent a long time in retreat, and for several months I looked into this question of my deepest willingness to be a human being. My central practice was this mantra:

> Anything that can happen to a human being may happen to me, and I accept the truth of this.

I would repeat it silently, while countless images and scenarios flitted across my mind—cancer, blindness, amputation, my wife or son being murdered, and so on. With each image, I silently, often with frightened surrender, bowed in acceptance of the possibility. It wasn't macabre or perverse at all; it was a quieting and deeply humbling process.

Obviously, I don't want any of those things to happen. But to be fully alive, to meet your life as a full human being, unafraid of reality and with both eyes wide open, you must accept the simple truth that anything that can happen to a human being may happen to you. You are a human being, so the statement is a literal truth. No way around it.

The practice helped me see countless sides of my relationship to life and, perhaps most important, discern the intricate balance between responsibility and surrender. There are many things we have control over and many things we have no control over. Spiritual practice gives us the opportunity to refine our understanding of which is which, and then to live accordingly.

To live accordingly means to practice the elements of what any culture would call a good and moral life—taking care of body, mind, and spirit, being kind and generous, not harming others, and so forth. By living in such a way, we dodge the sorts of calamities and dangers that are usually the result of irresponsible, lazy, or reckless living.

But living accordingly also means to accept the truth of the other part—that we never know, when we wake up in the morning, whether we will live to see the sunset or what shape we will be in by the end of the day. No amount of right living guarantees we will not be subject to disease, tornadoes, rape, murder, robbery, fire, car wrecks, humiliation, business failure, and so on.

To accept this fully not only is the essence of humility but also connects us deeply to every other living being, human and otherwise. These are the great equalizers, the things that are happening to somebody, somewhere, at every hour of night and day. This truth unites us all, and can give us compassion for all. No amount of wealth or social power can protect us from the natural forces of destiny.

So right living includes both the part we are responsible for, which can definitely shield us from unnecessary suffering such as addiction, many health problems, and many family and career problems; but it also includes the willingness to accept our share of "natural" misfortunes without crying "Why me?" There is always a simple answer to "Why me?": You are a human being, and this is one of the things that can happen to a human being. Why should it be anyone other than you?

I don't mean to imply that tragedies occur randomly. If faith means anything at all, it means there is order and intelligence in creation, and nothing befalls us without some purpose. This mantra, "Anything that can happen to a human being may happen to me, and I accept the truth of this," merely serves as a reminder that any imaginable event or condition may serve that highest purpose.

This practice can open up a deep level of honesty about life's realities while also gradually building our latent courage to face those realities as mature spiritual pilgrims. It is a great relief to wake up each morning not knowing what to expect, and to be at peace with that. It helps us cherish each other and our lives a great deal.

The universal truth of this mantra underlies the entire human experience. Our personal acceptance of it defines that experience as a spiritual adventure with meaningfulness from beginning to end. Our lives are no less of a heroic journey than the lives of Moses, Muhammad, Odysseus, Arjuna, Sita, Joan of Arc, or any other famed historical or legendary figures. We have what it takes to live fully and gloriously. But it does require steadfast willingness on our part to face life completely, without placing our demands on reality over what we will and will not accept.

> Anything that can happen to a human being may happen to me, and I accept the truth of this.

Lucky Breaks and Fractures

❧

I had been sort of busily coasting through life, when I was slammed up against an upsetting situation. I know I'm at a crucial crossroad, and how I handle this crisis will affect everything. How can I deal with a traumatic event?

The Talmud (a major reference work on the Jewish Torah) says that the reasons behind horrible events are not revealed to us. In a sense, the reasons are not our business. Our response is our business, and it may be the most important business of a lifetime. Talmudic scholars also say that we must thank God in advance for the gifts we are to be given, because most of the time we cannot recognize them as gifts when they arrive. They may seem like curses.

When I was eighteen years old, I fell asleep driving a compact car on a lonely stretch of highway in northern Florida and had a high-speed, head-on collision with a tractor trailer. The car virtually disintegrated. I fractured my skull, severed my upper gums, tore off a finger, crushed a spinal disc, burst my spleen, and took much of the glass from the windshield into my face. I pulled glass out of my face and arms for nearly two years afterward as shards moved their way toward the surface of the skin. I still carry scores of wire sutures inside my body, and steel pins have replaced some of the bones in my reattached finger.

My world was brought to a total stop. At that time, in 1965, I didn't know the language of wisdom traditions, but I knew instinctively that my life had changed forever. I dimly sensed that it might be up to me whether the change would turn out good or bad. Looking back now, I do have the words to describe it: a setback like that can either humble us or defeat us. This difference between humility and defeat is one of the most important life lessons I have come across.

Being humbled by the wreck would be to allow the shock, the life change, the pain, and the years of recuperation to open me up, make me more compassionate, more understanding, quieter, less selfish, less petty. Being defeated by it would be to allow myself to shut others out, develop bitterness and self-pity, become pettier and more demanding and angry. As I'm sure you've observed in your own life, defeat is often the first strong reaction to trauma or tragedy. We are tempted to shut down, get away, reject consolation or support, turn our fear and hurt into anger.

By some unseen grace, lying mangled in that hospital bed with tubes running in and out of every orifice, I gradually softened into humility rather than hardening into defeat. Images of my father, who had suffered a massive stroke at a relatively young age, kept appearing in the darkness of my nights. I could see on his face the dignity with which he bore his condition, the softness rather than hardness in his eyes.

Images of other disabled people, whom I had usually dismissed as irrelevant, also came into view. I realized that because of the damage to my face, now, and for the rest of my life, I might be someone most people avoided. Insensitive people might keep their children away from me or call me a freak, although I was still me behind all those injuries and scars. I felt sincere, tremendous remorse for being an ignorant, self-centered, vain person, and for growing up embarrassed about having a crippled father. I found myself sadly but firmly vowing to accept my lot whatever that might be. I decided to try to bring as much dignity to my condition as my father had brought to his.

I had no idea what that would entail, but some degree of peace crept into my life as I began to surrender to fate. I stopped worrying about the unknown limitations of my body or the likely repulsiveness of my face. Of course, even without any worries about the future, everything still hurt in nearly every part of my body for a long time. Physical pain became the center of my attention. I guess I felt that it was penance for a life lived so selfishly.

Yet at the same time, I had finally become a seeker of deeper truth. Something was strangely okay. After a few weeks, when I could speak, I repeatedly corrected anyone who referred to my "accident," preferring the word "wreck" instead. It did not make sense to me that anything so life-changing could be considered an accident. Something had happened. Despite the pain, it was at least partly something wonderful: I was finally on a journey toward a meaningful life.

I'm not suggesting that everyone requires as traumatic an awakening as I experienced. We all face the same choices of accepting or rejecting, being humbled or defeated, facing our challenges or running from them, whether the arena is a car wreck or a choice of a college major, a stillbirth or a change of careers. The principles play the same, however mild or intense our particular scenarios may be.

As Jesus pointed out in the Sermon on the Mount, there

is "the broad way which leads to destruction"—the path of least effort, least responsibility, least farsightedness, and therefore the most travelers. And there is the "narrow way which leads to life"—the harder choice, the greater effort, the swimming upstream against the world's current of fear and distraction. We cannot always choose what happens to us, but our lives will unerringly reflect our choices of response. However great our tragedies, we can choose a response that ennobles the human race rather than diminishes it, a response that humbles us rather than defeats us.

A Practice: MANTRAS FOR EVERYDAY LIFE

We may wish to maintain presence of mind when we are faced with a crisis or trauma, but how can we actually ensure it? How can we become people whose instantaneous reflexes turn to the spiritual rather than to fear, rage, or denial? One thing is for sure: we cannot wait until we are in times of crisis to develop a good crisis response. We must practice a spiritual focusing technique during ordinary times, so that when a crisis comes, it is almost second nature to respond from a centered place.

The Sanskrit word *mantra* is a combination of root words that together mean "mind protector." Mantra can be practiced on many different levels. A person may take one of the names of God as a mantra, for example, and try to repeat it silently throughout the day. This type of mantra practice can steady the mind in a devotional way.

Over a long period of time, mantra can strengthen one's focus to an extraordinary degree. Mahatma Gandhi used perhaps the most common Hindu mantra, *Ram* (God), for many years. When an assassin fatally shot him point-blank, the only thing he uttered as he crumpled to the ground was *"Jai Ram!"* Not "How could you?" or "No, no!" Just "Hail God." Imagine such unshakable presence of mind.

We can also use mantras as a practical tool for reminding ourselves of changes we're trying to make in our lives. They can help us break through old habits and limited ways of seeing things. The practice is separated into two parts: *investment* and *ropotition.*

1. Sit quietly with one of the following mantras in the morning and repeat it to yourself for at least ten minutes (longer if you can), letting the shades of meaning sink in deeper and deeper until you feel connected to what the mantra is saying to you personally. This is called investing a mantra.
2. After having invested the mantra, bring it to mind as often as you can throughout the day, especially as you get caught up in the conflicts or dramas of what's going on around you. Let the mantra remind you of your deeper view, your cosmic humor, or the depth you may have felt during the investment period. Let it help change your view right in the middle of all the action. It will if you stick with it.

Here are a few mantras to try, both classic and contemporary:

CLASSIC MANTRAS

The most traditional form of mantra is to repeat one of the names of God, or a sacred phrase containing holy words. The sages tell us that the sounds of such words alone, especially in ancient languages such as Arabic, Hebrew, and Sanskrit, cause vibrations that affect our bodies, minds, and spirits.

You can see if one of the following mantras calls to you, or just try one anyway for a month or so, and see how it feels. These classic mantras, as well as many others, can be repeated dozens or even thousands of times daily—waiting for a plane, at the grocery store, in a traffic jam, in times of fear or stress, and so on.

- *Jai Ram* or *Hare Krishna*. Both mean "Hail God" in Hindi. Longer versions of both, which are also used widely, are *Sri Ram Jai Ram Jai Jai Ram* and *Hare Krishna Hare Krishna, Krishna Krishna Hare Hare, Hare Ram Hare Ram, Ram Ram Hare Hare.*
- *Lord Jesus Christ, Son of God, have mercy upon me, a sinner.* This is called the "Jesus Prayer."
- *Om mani padme hum.* Tibet's mantra of compassion. Each of the six syllables is said to purify different levels of our being and to grant strong protection from negative influences and illnesses.
- *Baruch ata Adonai Eloheinu melech ha'olom.* "Blessed are You, oh Lord our God," in Hebrew.
- *La ilaha ill Allâh.* From the Muslim Koran, it means "None has the right to be worshipped but God."

CONTEMPORARY MANTRAS

- *It's good to be alive.* This is not so elementary as it may seem. To be alive, to be breathing, is good. Before anything is added that causes pleasure or pain, harmony or conflicts, comfort or fear, success or failure; before we are old or young, black or white, rich or poor, man or woman, imprisoned or free, *it's good to be alive.* In and of itself. For itself. Don't overlook it. Be grateful. If we let that most basic appreciation slide from our awareness, we will be endlessly batted back and forth like a Ping-Pong ball between happiness and sadness, loss and gain, pleasure and pain, constant change. The most effective way to deal with the world is to be firmly centered in life's free, basic, unchanging goodness.

In the investment period, repeat *It's good to be alive,* and gradually deepen your direct, gentle experience of being alive. Feel grateful. Bring a soft smile of wisdom into your heart to start the day, knowing that today will bring ups and downs like every other day, but you will try not to be a Ping-Pong ball.

- *One God.* Sita and I often invoke this mantra, as do other members of our community. When things do not go as they are supposed to go, it is useful to remember that there are not two Gods—one who sees your flat tire, and a different one who knows you are due at a meeting in ten minutes. *One God.* Whenever we feel torn between two apparently opposing forces or conditions, this mantra can help us accept the conflict and deal with it.

- *No hard feelings.* This mantra has been powerful for a lot of people. During the investment period, as you repeat it to yourself, see how many different types of hard feelings come to mind, from the minor ego bruises of yesterday at the supermarket, to the most serious grudges you have been holding since your childhood. Let them all go. Let even your enemies off the hook. Soften and depersonalize any emotional states that have caused you pain for so many years. Understand your past conflicts as though each one were a Superbowl game that you fought hard and lost. Let the opposing players off the hook; the game is over. Move on.

The more you see the truth of things, the easier it is to do whatever you need to do, but without self-righteousness, anger, or bitterness. Every time you feel a harsh feeling, a bitter edge, bring the mantra to mind. *No hard feelings.* It's tough sometimes, but it works.

- *Untouched.* During the investment period, while silently repeating *Untouched,* try to feel that central part of you that has always been the same, through every experience of your life—that inner, unchanging witness of every moment. That is the one true, immortal Self. Take a few moments to realize that this Pure Awareness has been exactly the same during the best and worst events of your life.

   Especially when you feel extremely caught, negative, or frightened, the mantra *Untouched* can help you remember that it is only the character you are playing who is caught or frightened, not the Actor. The Actor, Pure Awareness, remains untouched. This is a very good mantra for people who wish to be less touchy and temperamental. Your Real Self is beyond attack. As the Course in Miracles reminds us, "Nothing real can be threatened, nothing unreal exists."

Mantra practice may take some time to get used to. That's why it's called practice. You may look back on your day and realize that you forgot to use your mantra at all. Feel free to use any tricks you can think of to do better tomorrow. A rubber band around the wrist, a watch that beeps on the hour, whatever. Your ability to remember your mantra during the craziness of the day will strengthen greatly if you put in the effort.

I have practiced the mantra *Ram* for many years, and I am very comforted to see that even during dreams and nightmares, as well as real-life calamities, my mantra is right here, immediately reminding me to keep breathing, keep my faith strong, keep my mind clear and my heart open.

Do not make the mistake of thinking that the purpose of mantra is to tune yourself to a "higher plane" or in any other way remove you from the situation at hand. It is really the opposite: mantra helps you stay right here, with no need to run away; it helps you not waste time by resisting reality while also helping you respond deliberately with some degree of equanimity and gracefulness. Mantra is also a great substitute for unwanted stray thoughts and general noise of the mind. It is a very powerful life companion.

Our Cosmic Safety Net

❧

Once I've discovered the benefits of spiritual practice, how can I keep it up for the long haul? And how can I keep it moving deeper instead of slipping into just one more routine?

Any genuinely good life cannot be maintained without self-discipline and diligence, just as healthy teeth cannot be maintained without daily brushing. We don't consider brushing our teeth to be a serious intrusion on our time, or a dreaded period of our day. Every now and then we miss a time, but we're not always looking for excuses to miss brushing our teeth. Basically, we agree it is important, so we make it our own.

The first key to maintaining spiritual practice for the long haul is to deeply, deeply accept that spiritual practice is at least as important as brushing our teeth or taking showers or even drinking water. We must stop bucking, avoiding, making excuses, looking for ways out, looking for abstruse philosophies that suggest it is not important. We cannot see cavities developing, but we trust the dentists who tell us they will occur if we don't brush. Countless sages have advised us even more strongly toward spiritual practice. Do we want to trust dentists more than sages?

A devotee once complained to the great 19th-century saint Sri Ramakrishna about not having any deep experiences of God. Sri Ramakrishna took him by the hand and led him to the ashram's bathing ghat [pond]. They both walked into the water until they were about waist-deep, and Sri Ramakrishna then pushed the man's head under water with great force and held him there for nearly a minute. The man struggled and struggled, and finally the saint released his grip and the man emerged urgently from the water, gasping for breath. Sri Ramakrishna said to him, "When you want God as much as you wanted that next breath, you will see God."

I would love to want God as much as I want my next breath, wouldn't you? But for now, at least I do want to feel fairly confident that I am moving in the right direction. The most remarkable and inspiring people who have ever lived have been people of faith, so I choose to be a person of faith. They have been people who placed great importance on spiritual practice, so I choose to place great importance on spiritual practice. It's as simple as that.

Once we solidify our determination like this, then we can move on to the next part of the question: How can we go deeper and deeper, how can we want God more and more, until we do want God as much as our next breath? Among all spiritual practices, prayer is the very core practice for spiritual aliveness, for keeping things fresh and moving even deeper. Our prayer life can keep peeling away layers of inertia, self-deceit, insincerity. Prayer can keep us honest and humble. Prayer is our safety net from free will itself; it was designed into the equation right around the exit gate at the Garden of Eden. Adam and Eve didn't need prayer before they tasted of the fruit of knowledge of good and evil—in other words, before they had self-consciousness enough to exert free will. Up to that point, life was all God's will. Life and death unfolded in perfect harmony. But from the moment we became conscious of our nakedness, or separation from God's will, prayer was given to us as one way we could maintain at least a thread of our connection. Our Great Mission, as individuals and as a species, is to learn how to use our free will wisely enough to go full circle back into oneness with God. In other words, with beautiful poetic irony, the ultimate free-will decision is to give up our free will. *Thy will be done, Lord, on Earth* (here in my life, your life) *as it is in Heaven.* It's very clear.

A thumbnail sketch looks something like this: first there's God's will and no self-suffering; then there's man's will versus God's will, with plenty of self-suffering; and finally, after a long search for relief from pain, man's will again becomes the same as God's will—the end of self, the end of suffering. *The Kingdom of Heaven is at hand.* The choice has always been ours. That's the Great Problem, and that's the Great Solution as well.

Prayer and meditation are distinct. Prayer is a relationship with the Divine characterized by waiting and listening. Meditation is dissolving into the Divine beyond relationship, beyond identity. Praying as a spiritual practice is just that: practice. After enough practice, and as we become more mature, real prayer happens effortlessly all day long. Every moment of life becomes equally sacred and prayerful by nature. We come to a point where, as C. S. Lewis described, "There seems no center because it's *all* center."

Many of us tend to use prayer like a secret rabbit's foot, whipping it out when we need help with big problems. But every moment of our lives is truly the same size as every other. The seeker lives in prayer, rather than praying for this or for that. The wise rely on God for their very next breath.

Who is it that we pray to? And is it necessary to figure that out? Many people have no problem at all with their inner feelings about God, Christ, the Holy Spirit, the Great Spirit, Allah, Krishna, Rama, Buddha, or any other form to whom they address their prayers. But the rest of us are confused. After all, it's true that we're not really separate from God anyway. We're only under the illusion of separateness. So who or what is there to pray to other than our deepest selves?

Don't get lost in words and concepts. Prayer is simply a way of probing our connection to the forces behind the world, whatever anyone may wish to call them. Maybe we pray to ourselves; maybe we pray to the intelligence behind nature; maybe prayer is just a way of discovering some of our own hopes and fears. The answer doesn't really matter, because the bottom line is that prayer works in powerful ways. It may work in an entirely different way than what we thought we wanted; it may not even be recognizable in the way our answers come. But it works.

When we really get it right, praying is about the most intimate thing we could ever do. Besides calling on God, we're also exposing our innermost selves to ourselves. We discover our deepest hopes and fears, our basic innocence, and we prepare our subconscious minds for the major changes that are bound to occur during our spiritual journey.

We also may stop in our tracks in the middle of a prayer when we see how self-centered or limited our prayers sound to our hearts. Are we praying for our daughter to win the spelling bee, when millions of equally sweet children do not have enough to eat? Do we pray to be cured of cancer, rather than for faith and courage to handle whatever is meant to be? Does it sometimes happen that our genuine yearning to go deeper has devolved into neurotic whining instead? Daily practice of prayer can result in quite a bit of long-term spiritual therapy.

I love the openness and creativity of prayer. The only requisite is that it be genuine. We are not called by God to be anyone other than ourselves, as is wonderfully illustrated by the following story:

> There was once an illiterate cowherd who did not know how to pray, so instead he would say to God, "Master of the Universe, you know that if you had cows and you gave them to me to look after, I would do it for nothing, even though I take wages from everyone else. I would do it for you for nothing because I love you." A certain sage chanced upon the cowherd and heard him praying in this manner. The sage said to him, "You fool! You must not pray like that!". . . and set about teaching him the order of prayers as they are found in the prayerbook. After the sage went away, the cowherd soon forgot what he had been taught and so he did not pray at all. He was afraid to say his usual prayer about God's cows, because the sage had told him it was wrong to say such things; on the other hand, he could not say what the sage had told him because it was all jumbled up in his mind. That night the sage was reprimanded in a dream and told that unless the cowherd returned to his spontaneous prayer, great harm would befall the sage, because he had stolen something very precious away from God. On awakening, the sage hurried back to the cowherd and . . . begged him to forget what he

had told him and go back to his real prayers that
he had said before ever they had met.

—*The Way of the Jewish Mystics*

Praying for more devotion to God is one common form
of prayer that is actually answered in the very act of doing
it. The more we do it, the more time we are devoting to our
relationship with God. At some point in that relationship,
we begin to understand that what we think of as our yearning for God is actually God's yearning in our hearts for us
to pull closer and closer into that intimate relationship of
lover and beloved all day long.

A Practice: PRAYER

I find the best times of day for a formal practice of prayer are
at the end of each meditation period, when my mind is already relatively quiet. I pray spontaneously throughout the
day as well, but the formal periods are very helpful for beginning and ending my day. Prayer need not take a long time, but
it should be wholehearted. Take the time to grasp the content
of your prayers as fully as possible before moving on. My own
morning prayers include the specific members of my family
and community, plus others who have asked me to pray for
them, plus a heartfelt blessing to everyone, everywhere. This
reminds me of my aims in life.

Eventually, the words for most prayers will come freely out
of the depths of your own heart. The following prayers are offered merely as suggestions, as initial guides to point the way.

They can be repeated, imitated, changed, used, or discarded. You may wish to use one to start off a session of prayer, and then allow your own heart to take the lead. I often discover surprising insights about myself merely by listening to my own prayers.

> *God, help me to open to your power. Help me to open to my power. Help me even to pray to you. Please, come into my life, and fulfill the Sacred Promises you have made through the ages.*
>
> —Anonymous

> *Oh Great Spirit, Whose voice I hear in the winds, Life to all the world, hear me. I come before you, one of your many children. I am small and weak. I need your strength and wisdom. Let me walk in beauty and make my eyes ever behold the red and purple sunset. Make my hands respect the things you have made, my ears sharp to hear your voice. Make me wise, so that I may know the things you have taught my people, the lesson you have hidden in every leaf and rock. I seek strength not to be superior to my brothers, but to be able to fight my greatest enemy—myself.*
>
> *Make me ever ready to come to you with clean hands and straight eyes, So when life fades as a fading sunset, my Spirit may come to you without shame.*
>
> —Chief Yellow Lark

> *Lord, make me an instrument of Thy peace. Where there is hatred—let me sow Love;*

Where there is injury—Pardon;
Where there is doubt—Faith;
Where there is despair—Hope;
Where there is darkness—Light;
Where there is sadness—Joy.
O Divine Master, grant that I may not so much
    seek to be consoled, as to console;
To be understood, as to understand;
        To be loved, as to Love.
For it is in giving that we receive;
In pardoning that we are pardoned;
In dying that we are born to Eternal Life.

                                        —St. Francis

From the Unreal lead me to the Real.
From Darkness lead me to Light,
From Death lead me to Immortality.

                        —Brhadaranyaka Upanishad

My Lord Creator of all,
Master of all worlds.
Supreme, compassionate and forgiving,
Thank You for Your Torah,
Thank You for allowing me to learn from it
And to move toward serving You.
Thank You for revealing some of the
Mysteries of Your Way.
I'm amazed this is truly happening to me.

Please forgive my foolishness and unkindness,
The sins of my past.
Sincerely I pledge to live more uprightly

That I may be ever closer to You.
Fill me with that awe of You that
    opens my capacity
For loving.
And open my heart to the mysteries
    of Your Holy Way.
Reveal Your Torah, I pray.

—Jewish prayer

Lord, help me to keep my thoughts pure, my words
true, and my deeds kind; that alone or with others,
I shall be at one with thee. God, be in my mouth
and in my speaking. God, be in my heart and in
my thinking.

—Sarum Primer, 1558

O Thou, who are the perfection of Love, Harmony,
and Beauty, The Lord of Heaven and Earth, Open
our hearts that we may hear thy voice, which con-
stantly comes from within. Disclose to us Thy Divine
Light which is hidden in our souls, that we may
know and understand life better.
Most merciful and compassionate God, give us Thy
goodness. Teach us Thy loving forgiveness. Raise
us above the distinctions and differences which di-
vide us. Send us the peace of Thy Divine Spirit, and
unite us in Thy Perfect Being. So be it.

—Hazrat Inayat Khan

—May I be true today. May I be open. May I be
strong. May I be generous. May I be grateful. May
I laugh. May my life this day be of benefit to all be-
ings.

—May I live simply today, avoiding clutter and excess. May I tap my strengths and gain understanding of my weaknesses. May I support each person I meet in the sacred journey, for the benefit of everyone, everywhere.

—May I practice genuine, deep kindness and goodwill without limits. May I see through the illusions posed by selfish thoughts. May I experience the joy and freedom of cherishing others more than myself.

—Kindness House Morning Invocations

Take Off the Bumper Stickers

I have been teaching my children to be proud of themselves. I tell them how proud of them I am, so they'll have a lot of self-confidence. Why is pride considered a sin in the religious traditions?

No spiritual tradition has cautioned us against feeling the quiet self-confidence and self-respect that arise from living morally and being capable human beings. But America is the first society since the fall of Rome to consider personal pride a prized virtue instead of a dangerous vice. Pride is in, modesty is out. Aggressiveness is in, deference is out. Boastfulness is in, humility is out. Competitiveness is in, self-sacrifice is out. These are not components of a peaceful, friendly, cooperative nation. From any perspective of classic wisdom, we are skating on very thin ice.

We tell our children, "Oh don't be modest. You've got to shout, you've got to celebrate your gifts, child! The only way to get ahead is to blow your own horn. Always make sure you stand up for yourself. Don't take a back seat to anybody!"

Even if you and I try to make sure our own children pay some attention to community service or charitable works, it is important to acknowledge that our national child-raising strategy—the pervasive values imparted on television, in movies, and through the educational system to your kids as well as to anyone else—is currently set up to deliberately produce self-obsessed, aggressive, pushy human beings. The main thing we need to notice about this is that our nation's kids are not especially happy. In fact, as a generation, they are actually pretty angry, and becoming seriously violent at earlier and earlier ages. We urgently need to question our current assumptions and be willing to change them.

We're good people and we mean well, but we're not thinking clearly. We hear one "expert" say that kids need praise, and the next day somebody begins cranking out millions of bumper stickers saying "My child is an honor student at Smith Junior High." That's not praise, it's tacky boastfulness. It violates classic spiritual principles about humility and modesty, and it does not take the place of spending more time with our kids.

Children need to be appreciated a lot more than they need to be praised. Appreciation takes more time and commitment than praise. It's a lot more work than merely mouthing popular slogans to our kids every day or slapping one more bumper sticker on our car.

Appreciation joins and unites, while praise tends to separate and elevate. When we say, "Oh, sweetheart, I love spending time with you; I treasure you so much in my life," that's appreciation. It means a tremendous amount to our children without also making them feel superior to the kid next door.

When we merely throw praise around, or continually say "I'm so proud of you" as a sort of contemporary parenting mantra, it tends to sound empty after a very short time. Our children don't know what to make of it, because it seems unrelated to the reality of their constantly shifting moods and feelings about themselves. They cease to trust us, and then resentment builds because they feel they have lost one of their prime sources of honest feedback, which they need desperately to become decent adults.

Dr. Nathaniel Branden, the father of our modern self-esteem movement, tied his ideas very much into behavior and conscience. His original message was not just that self-esteem is important, which is the only part that seems to have taken root in the pop culture. The other half of the message was that we will have high self-esteem if we live virtuously and behave decently, and we will have low self-esteem if we do not. He said that the way to avoid feelings of guilt is to stop behaving selfishly and harmfully. Dr. Branden's ideas involved relationship, not unconditional self-approval in a vacuum.

Several hundred long-term psychological studies suggest that self-esteem curricula in the American educational system have been a colossal failure. Children have been taught to think highly of themselves no matter how they behave toward others. It's become an enormous mess. In one study, gang members scored highest on self-esteem questionnaires, because they stuck with their opinions and justified their feelings no matter what anyone else thought or how much anyone was harmed by their actions. They learned the curriculum well: they did not allow anyone to "run a guilt trip" on them for their behavior. They thought very highly of themselves, and that was all that mattered.

The studies also showed that high self-esteem was totally unrelated to improvement in grades or admirable performance in academics, sports, or music. What began as a reasonable idea—"Sweetheart, you can always hold your head high even if you are not the best in something"—has snowballed into "Kids, you should all feel equally good about yourselves whether you try or don't try, do your best or worst, act selfishly or unselfishly. None of that matters. All that matters is that you feel great about yourself." This is not natural, and that's why it doesn't work. Human beings are not going to feel good about themselves if they are lazy, spoiled, self-centered, greedy, and apathetic. Thank God! We're not supposed to feel good about ourselves if we're that way; that's nature's way of getting us to try to do our best and be our best. The human species would never have survived the process of evolution with the level of serious numbness and apathy that marks many of our children's basic attitudes today. A living being, of any species, must strive mightily to meet the challenges of nature. Rising to meet challenges is built into the code of all life forms.

We all have tremendous potential, and that potential will not manifest itself if we have no inner incentives. One of the most fundamental inner incentives is the feeling "I could have done better." If everyone around us rushes to say, "Oh no, no, don't say that; you did fine. You should feel wonderful about yourself for doing exactly as you did," then our most basic drive for excellence is quashed. We think we're being kind, but it is actually a very cruel thing to do to a child.

For nearly a full generation, we have imparted a message to our children that striving for excellence is unimportant. Maybe it is unimportant in terms of impressing others or being better than others; but the point we missed is that it is important to ourselves. Separating self-esteem from behavior and attainments has been an enormous mistake. Our society will be reaping the consequences of this mistake for many years.

And on top of these significant sociopolitical and psychological consequences, let's remember that the primary thrust of the spiritual journey—which is our children's ultimate task on earth as well as ours—is to move beyond ego altogether. God tells Moses, "No man sees my face and lives," reminding us that so long as we are in duality, so long as there are I and Thou, then we are not in true communion with the holiest of holies. In other words, we cannot "know" God, but we can merge into God. A cup of water cannot know the ocean, but when poured into the ocean, it becomes ocean.

Yogis, saints, sages, and gurus—human beings who reportedly live in or close to a God-realized state all the time—usually have extremely dynamic personalities and tremendous individuality, as well as merciless senses of humor. They have a natural self, but no self-consciousness, no self-esteem be it high or low. No inner voice is constantly saying, "How am I doing? Do they like me? Oh, I want that! I want to avoid that! How am I feeling? How am I feeling? How am I feeling?"

To grasp the incredible freedom and ease of an egoless self, consider how the senses and organs work. Eyes and ears perform complex processes constantly. They are extremely active, extremely sensitive, extremely tuned into the present moment in very dynamic ways. Yet there is no self-consciousness in them at all, no ego-voice saying to the eyes, *Okay, the light flow is fading 13 percent, so open up the cones and shut the rods a little; that's good, that's good; oh you are such good eyes, I really love— Damn you, why didn't you see that branch we just tripped over! Oh, here comes the mailman, adjust the cornea for distance, hold steady, that's good, now zoom in to his hand to see whether that's something for us he's holding . . .*

Think about the countless complex systems and processes in our brains and bodies that comprise our experience of the world, all functioning without such a pesky ego judging, cheering, or carrying on endless chatter. From my own experiences of Communion, I am certain that the mind and personality do not need to be driven by an ego any more than the eyes or ears or stomach or heart do.

Ego is not Self, it just pretends to be. Without ego, there's still someone who likes chocolates or avoids cooked carrots, who cusses up a storm or speaks very gently, still someone who represents a unique snowflake of God's power operating through one individuated form. Our senses and organs are unselfconsciously brilliant. An egoless state of mind is no less. It is spontaneous genius spilling out in every direction. That is why Tukaram, a seventeenth-century Hindu saint, exclaimed, "The death of the ego is a festive occasion beyond compare!"

We cannot pretend to be beyond ego. But it is important to have some idea of the egoless state in the back of our minds so that we do not solidify the role of ego any more than necessary. Ego is like a cocoon that protects us during a certain stage of growth toward becoming a butterfly. We can try to have a reasonably healthy ego structure, and help our kids to have reasonably healthy ego structures, without forgetting that it will be wonderful to someday fly free of that cocoon altogether. This is a proper balance of big view and small view.

A Practice: A PRAYER OF HUMILITY

A book about the late Mother Teresa of Calcutta and her Missionaries of Charity describes some of the prayers they have used in their spiritual practice. One, called the Litany of Humility, is especially powerful in balancing the ego-obsessed messages of modern life. Be forewarned—this is a radical and extremely difficult prayer to utter sincerely, because it goes so much against the grain of everything we are taught about self-care. As much as I love it, it still shakes me up even to read it, let alone to utter it with conviction.

I urge you to spend time with this prayer, not just to read it once or twice. Reflect on each line and notice any confusion or resentment that it brings up in you. Perhaps work with it every morning for a month. And try to remember that its purpose is grand and glorious freedom and joy, not any sort of masochism or self-defeat. Its purpose is to fly free from the cocoon and to rise into the heavens.

Deliver me, O Jesus,

From the desire of being loved,
From the desire of being extolled,
From the desire of being honored,
From the desire of being praised,
From the desire of being preferred,
From the desire of being consulted,
From the desire of being approved,
From the desire of being popular,
From the fear of being humiliated,
From the fear of being despised,

From the fear of suffering rebukes,
From the fear of being calumniated,
From the fear of being forgotten,
From the fear of being wronged,
From the fear of being ridiculed,
From the fear of being suspected.

That others may be loved more than I, Jesus grant
*   me the grace to desire it.*
That others may be esteemed more than I,
That, in the opinion of the world, others may in-
*   crease and I may decrease,*
That others may be chosen, and I set aside,
That others may be praised, and I unnoticed,
That others may be preferred to me in everything,
That others may become holier than me, provided
*   that I may become as holy as I should.*

Our modern minds may chafe at the idea of giving up the desire to be loved or the fear of being humiliated. We say, "But
isn't that just natural? Doesn't everyone want to be loved, and
want not to be humiliated?" Sure, everyone who's willing to
live forever in the cocoon.

Spiritual teachings are not the psychology of the world.
They are recipes for a fundamental transformation of who we
think we are. If we truly let go of every one of the desires and
fears mentioned in her prayer, we would no longer be "me,"
we would be the love of God itself manifesting through a particular body and personality. Mother Teresa knew what she
was praying for. This prayer may be far beyond our current
reach, but it can be a powerful tool for remembering where
we're headed.

But Enough About Me

❧

I believe in silent spiritual practice, and I also believe it is imperative to work on my own self-esteem and to instill genuine self-esteem in my kids. Isn't a joyful life linked directly to feeling good about ourselves on all levels?

I'm all in favor of a joyful life. In my view, it will not come about by working on self-esteem directly. Call me old-fashioned, but I can't shake thousands of years' advice about the spiritual dangers inherent in esteeming ourselves. Even the phrase "working on self-esteem" is suspicious: Why does it take work at all to feel good about ourselves if we're living right?

As I mentioned in the preceding chapter, Nat Branden, the father of our modern self-esteem movement, never intended for self-esteem to become so isolated and individualistic. To him, self-esteem had everything to do with how we live in community with others.

In other words, true self-esteem is like a smile: it arises naturally in a life lived well. We don't stand in front of the mirror all day working on our smile. We don't wake up in the morning thinking "Now, let's see; I've got to smile today; I've got to smile. . . ." We do not have school curricula based on learning to smile, nor do we go to weekend smile workshops. Countless occurrences effortlessly bring a smile to our faces—nice people, a beautiful sky, a sweet cat or dog, a little baby, children playing, our old jalopy starting right up instead of our having to drag out the jumper cables.

Smiling is natural unless we allow ourselves to sink into despair for one reason or another. And if that were to happen, the solution would not be to practice smiling in and of itself, but rather to acknowledge the sources of despair and change them. Then, smiling will once again be part of our lives.

Self-esteem (actually, I greatly prefer "self-respect," but I will use the popular term for the sake of discussion) and simple joy function in the same way. The more we chase them, the further they recede; yet they are gifts that come to us when we give up self-absorption. Mother Teresa didn't undertake her mission in order to boost her self-esteem or to attain self-centered happiness. She followed her heart; she did what she felt was right. She dedicated her life to helping others. The result? A profoundly happy, joyful person, naturally esteemed by the whole world. How did she feel about herself? I doubt that question ever crossed her mind. She certainly laughed a lot, though, and seemed to squeeze every drop of preciousness from her life. According to Mother Teresa, "We belong to the whole world, living not for ourselves but for others."

America's reigning love affair with building self-esteem works in exactly the opposite direction: it's always about me, me, me. Our modern world is hooked on "looking out for number one," yet the more we do it, the more insecure we feel. So we increase the dosage: we pay even more attention to ourselves. It's a classic pattern of addiction, which does not yield a radiant, joyful human being. It's a flawed strategy based on a false premise—the notion that we are so small, so fragile, that we need propping up or boosting in the first place.

In most of us, there is indeed a discouraging little voice inside saying things like "You're no good; you'll never change; you're a big phony," and so forth. As it became increasingly clear in contemporary psychology how crippling that voice can be, a popular strategy evolved to drown out that little voice with a bigger voice saying things like "I'm special; I deserve happiness; I choose prosperity; I can accomplish whatever I set my sights on," and so forth.

The problem with that strategy is twofold:

1. High self-esteem is not the solution to low self-esteem; it is merely its other face. They are the two equal sides of excessive ego. A flood can drown you whether its waters are cold or hot. Egotism describes a *degree* of self-concern, not whether that concern is positive or negative.

2. When the mind becomes a battleground between those two voices, the inner detractor and the fervent cheerleader, there is no peace and quiet left. As most of us have seen if we're willing to admit it, it takes a tremendous amount of energy to keep propping up such an insecure ego. Aren't you weary of it by now?

I prefer another strategy: learning how to quiet down. In this manner, over a period of time, it is possible to observe and then dismantle that false negative voice at its source, so that you are left with no voices inside at all—just a calm human being with neither cheerleaders nor detractors vying for constant attention. Doesn't that sound more appealing? I assure you, it yields an enormous amount of energy for the real business of life.

When we begin to care more about others than about ourselves—what early Christians called self-forgetfulness and what Buddhists call *bodhicitta*—the joy we feel is mainly a sense of relief more than anything else. It's a happy relief to step aside from the spotlight of ego's endless desires and fears and self-analysis. It's a happy relief to open ourselves to what we are really and truly about—love, compassion, courage, kindness, mercy, dedication—instead of being constantly wrapped up in the newest scratch on the door of the minivan.

Joy is our natural state when we live a soul-centered, altruistic lifestyle. Life will provide natural self-respect and self-confidence if we but play by the rules set down through the ages. The very idea of esteeming ourselves is beneath our dignity when we begin to see who we really are and how profoundly we are all connected.

A Practice: AN EXERCISE IN SEEING

It is easy to talk about seeing this and seeing that, or to say, "Oh, I see your point," and so forth. But do we really see? In the paragraph above, I said, "when we begin to see who we truly are and how profoundly we are all connected." I meant that literally, not just as a way of saying "when we begin to *understand* who we are . . ." I meant that we can actually learn to see others in an entirely different way. It just takes practice.

This exercise requires a partner and takes about twenty

minutes. There are many variations, but the point of them all is to learn how to see ourselves and others more clearly, past the usual fronts. The rules are: No talking, smiling, touching, laughing. Use only your eyes. This may feel embarrassing at first, but it's definitely worth getting past any initial awkwardness.

1. One variation is simply to sit across from each other as close as possible without your knees or any other body parts touching. Both partners look directly into each other's eyes for however long it seems productive. What you are looking for is your own self reflected in the other—a person who embodies the entire range of human feelings and yearnings and uncertainties, just like you. It usually takes about five minutes before we're able to drop our defenses and mental noise, so give it enough time. To end the practice, bow in appreciation to your partner for helping you better understand yourself.

2. Another variation is for you to start with eyes open while the other person keeps his or her eyes closed. Take this rare opportunity to study the other person without self-consciousness. Look into his or her face, look for the clues that reveal more than this person usually shows—traces of sadness, hope, fear, loss; having loved somebody who died, or who left. We've all experienced these things, so find it in your partner's face. And then realize it shows in yours too, and it's all right.

Continue looking for traces or clues from your partner that help you realize how similar life has been for both of you. The details may be different, but the feelings and experiences are so much the same! As you see them in your partner, reflect them in yourself too; this includes the big, invisible question mark we all have hanging over our heads as we keep guessing our way through life without truly understanding what's going on. See that this is the same for both of you, and for everyone.

Allow your heart to soften and your compassion to grow as you keep seeing these things in your partner. Allow it to beam out from your eyes so that you're bathing in him or her in love, just as if you were a saint looking at this person in front of you. You don't have to "try" to do anything; just get your ego out of the way and let God's love shine through your eyes.

Now softly say, "Okay," and your partner opens his or her eyes and looks straight into the eyes of God (*your* eyes) to receive all your compassion, understanding, and forgiveness. Your partner can let go of pain, guilt, shame and secrets through his or her eyes, letting them burn in the purifying fire of your compassion, without a word ever being spoken.

After two or three minutes, you both close your eyes, get centered, and when your partner feels ready you then repeat the whole practice, reversing the roles. When you're done with both rounds, sit and look at each other openly for a minute or so. End the practice by bowing in appreciation to your partner for helping you better understand yourself.

This practice can yield many psychological and emotional insights, but don't stop there. You can actually experience a merging into the other, a cessation of "small self" entirely, if you become open and willing enough to really enter into the heart of the practice. When Jesus said, "Love thy neighbor as thyself," he was pointing to a mystical truth as much as to a social one. This exercise in seeing can lead to quite a revelation that your neighbor is indeed none other than yourself.

It Always Gets Back to Kindness

I have friends who do plenty of spiritual practice, attend retreats, travel to the East, and who don't seem any more fulfilled than I am without doing any of those things. What are they missing? What should the end product look like when you are living a meaningful life?

In an interview toward the end of his life, Aldous Huxley was asked, "Dr. Huxley, perhaps more than anyone else in the world, you have studied all the great religions and spiritual traditions; can you summarize for us what you feel you have learned?" Huxley replied, "I think just to be a bit kinder."

Sita and I heard that remark quite a few years ago, and as we've gotten older it has sunk deeper and deeper into our hearts. For all our seeking and exploring, this simple, ageless wisdom remains the essence of a successful life on earth, no matter what convuluted paths we may take to learn it. And we have all day long, wherever we are, to practice it.

It is certainly possible to make spiritual seeking merely one more frenetic, object-oriented pursuit that may take us to the far reaches of the globe, but fails to fully open our hearts or to get our attention off ourselves. But like the old

Sufi saying goes, "There would be no counterfeit if real gold did not exist." There certainly is a way of seeking and practicing that results in profound transformation. And the transformed "us" does not necessarily look or behave in complex or esoteric ways. We may just be genuinely kinder.

There is no spiritual practice more profound than being kind to one's family, neighbors, the cashier at the grocery store, an unexpected visitor, the person who does the laundry or picks up the garbage, or any other of the usually "invisible" people whose paths we cross in the course of a normal day.

Certainly there are spiritual mysteries to explore, and states of ecstasy or enlightenment beyond description. But as we mature, it becomes clear that those special experiences are meaningful only when they arise from and return to a life of ordinary kindness. Whether we're sitting in silent meditation on top of a mountain, operating a drill press in a steel factory, or feeding the hungry in Ethiopia, a feeling of genuine kindness in our hearts is the practical expression of any spiritual path. When his disciples asked Jesus how people would recognize them as true Christians, he replied, "Love one another as I have loved you. That's how people will know you follow me."

In February of 1994, Sita and I had the opportunity to visit the Dalai Lama at his home in India. The Northern Himalayan village of Dharamsala is home in exile to thousands of Tibetan refugees who have fled the Chinese occupation of their country. One of the most inspiring things about spending a week in Dharamsala was the aliveness of religious practice there. Most of the population are Buddhist monks and nuns, and the Dalai Lama is their single, uncontested highest living saint; he's right there, preaching kindness and joy as the most important duties of life. It's like a Christian being in Jerusalem with Jesus living in the little place up the hill.

Even walking down the street in Dharamsala becomes a very happy experience. People are bowing almost constantly, exchanging greetings of *Tashi Deleg* (loving-kindness) with nearly everyone they see. The most practical thing is to keep your hands pressed together in *pranam* (respectful greetings), that's how constant the salutations of goodwill are.

Sita and I were blessed to have an hour-long meeting with His Holiness, who had invited us to India to discuss our work with prisoners. During our meeting, I put all my attention into being present, open, and receptive in the company of such a great spiritual elder. I tried to look at him objectively—"He's got two legs, two arms, a head, a nose. We both wake up in the morning, both go to sleep at night. What is the real functional difference between his experience of life and mine?"

One of the things I realized is simply that he's "full-time." You and I may go to a church service or a spiritual retreat, and with enough mutual support and encouragement, we may let down our guard and be willing to feel the Living Spirit with each other. We may be willing to be open and trusting, experiencing the preciousness of being together and practicing together. Then the service ends, and on the way home we stop for gas, or a bagel or something. And here is the difference: you and I are usually willing to be what Ram Dass calls "phony unholy" with the gas station attendant or the cashier. We won't look in his or her eyes. We turn away. We won't be intimate. It's like an unspoken agreement to avoid feeling how precious we are to each other. It would be too embarrassing to greet everyone we meet as sacred companions.

The Dalai Lama, and other saints like Mother Teresa and Mahatma Gandhi, simply don't turn it off! They go into the station and see a Precious Child of God taking their Divine Credit Card for the Sacred Gas, and they don't hide it! Their whole presence says, "Isn't this thrilling, to meet each other?" Getting gas, praying in church, buying a bagel, are all the same Mysterious Miracle. They live in Love, so of course they are in Love with the gas station attendant. Where else could they be? And at the bagel shop, they're in Love with the bagel boy.

You and I may not yet be saints. But that's no reason to shirk our spiritual responsibilities by saying only the few saintly people in the world can act like that. Jesus enjoined us, "Strive to be perfect, as your Father in heaven is perfect." Striving toward sainthood, toward perfection, is exactly what we're supposed to be doing. I know that sounds pretty heady and downright dangerous. Who do we think we are, to strive for perfection? But consider the opposite question: Who are we not to?

ACT GREAT

*What is the key to untie the knot of your
    mind's suffering?
What is the esoteric secret to slay the crazed one
    whom each of us did wed
and who can ruin our heart's and eyes' exquis-
    ite, tender landscape?
Hafiz has found two emerald words that re-
    stored me*

that I now cling to as I would sacred tresses of
my beloved's hair:
Act great. *My dear, always act great.*
What is the key to untie the knot of the mind's
suffering?
Benevolent thought, sound and movement.
   —Hāfiz (fourteenth-century Sufi poet),
   The Gift

A *Practice:* SETTING THE STAGE FOR A LIFE OF LOVINGKINDNESS

Occasionally we hear of a "Kindness Day" or even a "Kindness Week" in a particular town or city, when people try to perform what have been called random acts of kindness for friends and strangers throughout the day. This is a very sweet gesture and a nice community event. But a life of lovingkindness such as the saints and sages exemplify is a whole different thing. It is not just about being safely nice while everyone around us is also being nice.

A life of lovingkindness in the face of every day's events, good and bad, requires persistence and practice and a good deal of understanding. Here are two ways to begin setting the stage:

1. Commit at least one evening per month to watching a video about the life of a sage or saint. There are wonderful, deeply inspiring movies or documentaries available on Mother Teresa, the Dalai Lama, Father Bede

Griffith, Mahatma Gandhi, Ananda Mayi Ma, Ramana Maharshi, Peace Pilgrim, "The Man Who Planted Trees," and many others whose lives took on the very essence of kindness and compassion.

- Video is a powerful medium for inspiring us. Viewing one a month is like taking a monthly spiritual vitamin to remind us that a life of kindness is both possible and compelling.
- Do not combine viewing with popcorn and banter as though it were just any leisure-time video rental. Respect this time as a quiet and focused practice to bring your heart into the presence of the heart of God.
- If you watch with family or friends, try to have sincere discussion afterward about how best to integrate the sage's example into your own lives, however modestly. Acknowledge ways in which each of you tends to be kind and unkind. Resolve to make one change, no matter how small, or to perform one act of unreciprocated kindness, however modest, as a direct result of each video you watch.

2. Take the following vow each morning as part of your daily practice: *I will refrain from blaming others for my negative states of mind. I will refrain from blaming circumstances for my negative states of mind.*

- This is a vow that is popular in my community because of its power to break lifelong patterns of connecting irritability, depression, or anger with anyone or anything outside ourselves. Freeing ourselves from this tendency to blame is a great delight, and is essential for developing true lovingkindness. The notion that a bad night's sleep, or a physical illness, or a rude sales clerk has the power to depress or anger you is a false notion. It is within your power to dispel this false notion and take full responsibility for your states of mind. Perhaps no other story in history illustrates this better than the stoning of Saint Stephen. While an angry mob was stoning him to death for being a Christian, Stephen looked up and cried out, "Father, please do not hold this against them!" His lovingkindness was not dependent on anything outside himself. That's the only way lovingkindness can be complete. An American saint, a woman who called herself simply Peace Pilgrim, walked across the United States with no possessions other than the clothes on her back and a toothbrush in her bag. She was an embodiment of lovingkindness to such an extent that when a deranged young man attacked her and beat her viciously on the head and face, she would not even lift her hands to fend off his blows. She just stood there and looked at him with such compassion that he fell at her feet crying.

• You and I may be some distance away from being able to respond like Saint Stephen or Peace Pilgrim in life-threatening situations. But we have a clear opportunity today to begin with the most mundane examples of blaming our moods on others, and slowly work our way up to sainthood from there. My daughter-in-law, after working with this practice for only a few weeks, remarked that it had completely changed the nature of arguments between herself and my son. With no one to blame, ill will cannot escalate so quickly. We have more opportunity to hear each other's point of view and work out reasonable solutions. Even one person working with this vow changes the dynamic for both people in an argument.

• Our negative states of mind also tend to pass much more quickly when we are unable to pin them on others. We gain a finer understanding of the workings of human emotional states, which increases our empathy for others and spurs us on to greater lovingkindness.

This section of the book has dealt mostly with the personal transformation needed to experience Communion with the great spiritual force that resides within us. Many ideas and practices have been discussed, but it is good to keep a simple overview: we have something wonderful to awaken within us. It may take work, it may put us through all sorts of seemingly complex processes, but the goal of Communion is itself very straightforward and beyond our concepts and understandings. One of my favorite stories exemplifies this point in a delightful way:

> Abba Lot went to see Abba Joseph and said to him, "Abba, I fast a little, I pray and meditate, I live in peace and as far as I can, I purify my thoughts. What else can I do?" Then the old man stood up and stretched his hands towards heaven. His fingers burst into flame like ten lamps of fire and he said, "Why not change entirely, into fire?"
>
> —*Story of the Desert Fathers*

As we begin to commune with, or awaken, this wonderful, in-comprehensible spirit within us, the most natural thing in the world is to share our joy and gratitude with others through acts of compassion and kindness. This is the simple basis of all the chapters on Community, which follow in Part Two.

· Part Two ·

THE OUTER PATH

TOWARD COMMUNITY

Practicing Service

This is the true joy of life, the being used up for a purpose recognized by yourself as a mighty one; being a force of nature instead of a feverish, selfish little clod of ailments and grievances, complaining that the world will not devote itself to making you happy.

I am of the opinion that my life belongs to the community, and as long as I live, it is my privilege to do for it whatever I can. I want to be thoroughly used up when I die, for the harder I work, the more I live.

—George Bernard Shaw

A sense of community is part of our deepest nature. We are born into a family that lives within a tribe, village, town, or city. When drought or hurricanes or floods come, they affect our neighbors as well as us, and we are reminded of our need to help each other and to care for each other's well-being. As infants and children, we all develop natural self-ishness to some degree, but it remains very important to us to feel a sense of community and a sense of our own place in it.

In fact, approval and disapproval by others become significant mitigators of our natural selfishness, and that is entirely appropriate, so long as approval does not become our sole motivational system. We are individuals, but we are also communal human beings. These two roles are not at odds; rather, they provide crucial checks and balances for each other.

Service and community are inextricable. Service, in the largest sense, could be defined simply as the manifestation of our inborn concern for the common good. If we do not allow our desires and fears to get out of hand, we do naturally care about the welfare of others—others in our family, our community, our nation, our world. Because this is natural, it leads to happiness and meaningfulness. If we allow ourselves to be led astray by the competitive individualism of our day, so that all our attention is focused on our own wants and needs and goals, then we will not be happy no matter how much material success we achieve.

From this point of view, service and the pursuit of happiness are intimately linked. A classic Tibetan way of putting this is, "All suffering comes from cherishing ourselves more than others. All happiness comes from cherishing others more than ourselves." In other words, though we naturally have both selfish and altruistic leanings, we are advised to put the altruistic first if we know what's good for us. Jesus echoed this advice when he said, "Greater Love hath no man than this: That he lay down his life for his fellow man." Note the words "Greater Love." It stands to reason that a person feeling such great love would tend toward the happy and meaningful side of life. Note also that laying down our lives need not be confined to taking a bullet for somebody but may simply be another way of agreeing with George Bernard Shaw that "my life belongs to the community."

If, like Shaw, our inner attitude is that we belong to each other, then service and marriage, service and family life, service and personal success, service and good citizenship need not create conflict for us. We need to take care of ourselves in order to be of optimal service. We need to have fun, to take vacations, enjoy an occasional lazy day in order to be in the best shape for others afterward. The ancient Israelites did not bring diseased or blemished lambs to the altar; they brought their very best. If we aim to place ourselves on the altar of life as a gift to the world, then we need to take proper care of ourselves so that we can be the best gift possible.

But we also need to remember that altruism must ultimately be altruistic, not merely a strategy for personal happiness. Rabbi Benjamin Twerski, in his book *Not Just Stories,* recounts a pithy Hasidic tale to this effect:

> A woman once came to the Maggid of Kozhnitz asking for his blessing for a child, since after a number of years of marriage, she and her husband were still childless. The Maggid replied, "My parents, too, were childless for many years. Then my mother sewed a coat for the Ba'al Shem Tov, and after that I was born."
>
> The woman exclaimed, "I will gladly sew a coat for you, a beautiful coat!" The Maggid

shook his head. "No, my dear woman," he said. "That will be of no avail. You see, my mother did not know this story."

TIKKUN

Tikkun is a Hebrew word that is often translated as "world repair." To me, tikkun is not just about external service; it starts in our most basic, almost instinctual view of being involved with life as a helper. The Maggid's mother in the story above probably saw that the Ba'al Shem Tov did not have a suitable coat, and regardless of her own problems, a spirit of tikkun naturally moved her to make him one. She contributed to life by making a coat for a holy man, so life then contributed to her in the form of her pregnancy. Most of us have experienced this phenomenon at some time or other; we let go of self-interest and then discover, usually to our surprise, that our interests have been provided for anyway. The sages are merely exhorting us to live in such a way more and more: give our lives to the common good, and see whether life takes care of us.

This spirit of tikkun is the essence of compassionate service—not how much good we do, but rather waking and sleeping, eating and breathing, working and playing, with an unforced, underlying attitude of goodwill; no time off. When we leave from our volunteer stint at the orphanage or the soup kitchen or the AIDS hospice and stop off at the grocery store on the way home, we must understand that noticing the cashier as a human being is as significant as whatever noble cause we just volunteered for. It is nothing short of barbaric to deal with as many human beings as most of us deal with every day and have as little real human contact as many of us do. (See the "Civilizing Your World" Practice on page 131.)

Until we take such simple personal responsibility for cherishing others all day long, our sociopolitical accomplishments will be fleeting and fragile. We can easily see proof of this by looking at the past forty years in both America and the rest of the world. Americans waged a war on poverty, passed a landmark civil rights bill, and made unbelievable advances in medicine and technology. Yet today our prisons are overflowing; streets and parks in all major cities abound with homeless men, women, and children; gated communities patrolled by armed guards are no longer only for the superwealthy but have actually become a popular type of subdivision.

These are just a few of the human elements of the modern equation, and in these ways, despite computers and cell phones and all the rest, we may be at an all-time low point in our national community. From those gated subdivisions to the most massive prison buildup the world has ever known, consider how much energy we spend trying to keep other human beings out of our lives. This is a very shortsighted approach to personal security. It is not the way of tikkun, it is not the way of community or service, and it will not lead us to a period of peace and prosperity.

Sometimes we can make the opposite mistake as well: those of us who devote our lives to serving the poor can erect just as many walls against our sense of community with the middle class and the wealthy. Many seekers in the 1960s, including Sita and myself, experienced profound communion through our various wholehearted explorations, but most of us got only half the picture. We touched some deep places of spirit internally that inspired us to identify with minorities, poor people, indigenous peoples, gypsies, and outlaws and outcasts, but we failed to recognize the very same holy spirit reflecting through what we derisively called the "straight world"—mainstream society. We were on to something, but fell far short of a mature realization that would make the whole world our family. Our world was still divided into "us" and "them," which is like having half a million-dollar bill: it holds the promise of immense wealth, but is worth zero by itself. The two halves must be brought together to constitute a true fortune.

SEEKING A WAY OF LIVING: PROCESS VERSUS OBJECT ORIENTATION

I once counted that in the first five years Sita and I were married, we lived in twenty-four different places. Not just different places, but radically different environments—urban, rural, wilderness, sailboats, farms, trailers, alone, communally. There was no perfect situation that automatically brought our lives into harmony with all of creation. We finally began to understand that the truth we were seeking was not to be found merely in one set of conditions over another, but rather in a way of seeing and responding to any conditions, anywhere. In other words, we had been seeking a way of life (object), when the answer was actually to practice a way of living (process).

Both Hasidic Jewish and Tibetan Buddhist traditions give the example of a traveler checking into a hotel room for one night, and spending thousands of dollars to redecorate the room. In other words, we expend our soul-energy on senseless object orientation, and then when it's time to check out, we feel like fools for forgetting that we were only passing through. We are on a grander journey than the one defined by the color of our curtains or the size of our TV screen.

For example, each day when you go to work, the object is arriving at work, while the process includes every moment of getting there. If you are stuck in object orientation, then the journey is meaningless to you; it's a big waste of time or even a barely tolerable, stress-building exercise in frustration—traffic jams, rude drivers, unreliable trains, smelly buses. Take young children along with you on that same trip, and you will witness nonstop interest in the weather, the many faces and sights you see on the way, birds and clouds, the feelings in their own bodies, all sorts of phenomena that children naturally find fun and fascinating. As one master said, "Boredom is merely a lack of attention."

The spiritual principle of process orientation, sometimes called mindfulness, means, like a child, you allow yourself to be 100 percent engrossed in the journey itself, then 100 percent engrossed in your day at work, then 100 percent engrossed in the journey home, and then 100 percent engrossed with your family. Life becomes a moving fullness rather than a series of intervals between "important" and "unimportant," "relevant" and "irrelevant." Every moment is important and relevant to a mind unburdened with ceaseless objects and concepts.

When the great Eastern European Rabbi Moshe of Kobryn died in 1858, his chief disciple was asked, "What was the most important thing to your master?" His immediate reply was, "Whatever he happened to be doing at the moment." This in some ways is the pivotal spiritual practice around which all others revolve: to honor and care for all of creation all the time. This is process orientation. It is a reminder that every moment has equal meaning; a reminder to be fully aware and respectful at all times. We slip a dollar to a panhandler, or thank the cashier at the grocery store, or patiently respond to a stranger's request for directions downtown. We begin to hear Jesus say, "Inasmuch as you did these things for the least of my brethren, you did them for me." Imagine the juiciness of a life in which every moment and every person is equally sacred!

NO EXCUSES

In every world religion, the importance of community is clear. Once again, the holy teachings have expressed universal ethics and standards for human behavior:

> Be kind to one another.
> Love thy neighbor as thyself.
> Do unto others as you would have them do unto you.
> Be hospitable to strangers, for you were once a stranger yourself.
> Serve the poor; make the world a better place.

This is not a vague area of doctrine, it's crystal-clear. Jesus even went so far as to make sure his disciples realized that when they fed *any* beggar or visited *any* prisoner or clothed *any* naked person, they fed and visited and clothed him. I also love the clever way Lao-Tzu expressed the principle of community about five hundred years before the Christian era:

> The first practice is the practice of undiscriminating virtue: Take care of those who are deserv-

ing. Also, and equally, take care of those who are
not.

If we pay attention to these ancient teachings, we have no
excuses for mistreating or neglecting anyone. It's easy to
think of family and friends as community, and everyone
else as strangers, associates, rivals, or even enemies we must
cope with in order to make a living, commute to work, get
ahead, and so on. It's also easy to think, "I'll practice community as soon as I get home from work, as soon as my kids
are grown, as soon as my boss stops picking on me, as soon
as I get out of debt, as soon as . . ."

But life doesn't work that way. Our community is exactly
where we are at every moment during the day; exactly
whom life places in front of us at any time. That's the whole
point. The boss who drives us up the wall, the windbag
politician on TV, the incompetent store clerk—everyone
we see, hear, or meet must be respected as a brother or sis-
ter on the path, whether our respect is reciprocated or not.

Clearly, this practice of community and service to others
is not for cowards; it's challenging and confusing, and it's
full-time. No one else in the world can play our unique
role. God knows where we are, knows our needs and hopes
and dreams, depression or anxiety, the people we face, our
weaknesses, our fears and doubts. In a way, these very
crosses we bear are our credentials for being in community
with the equally flawed people all around us. We're all
trapped in an elevator together, and everyone is looking for
reassurance from those of us who can manage to be calm
and kind under the circumstances. If we help even one person or creature to feel safer or more loved today, we will
have been of service.

Ironically, this practice of true community may be at

times a lonely pursuit. Few of us are ever in the ideal situation where everyone around us changes at the same time, or all the rules suddenly become fair. Most of the time we have to start this humble hero's journey by ourselves, with little or no support. But then we receive the invisible support of Truth itself, because Community is a truer way of life than fear and selfishness.

The topics and practices here in Part Two may be challenging to some readers. I honestly feel that the deterioration of our national community means we must be willing to make some bold, occasionally painful changes. An alarming percentage of our population, of all ages, is taking antidepressants. At least one company is marketing peppermint Prozac for children. On the whole, our children's generation is not thriving. We must be willing to make some big changes.

The sages would always advise us to chart a course toward a less materialistic and more fulfilling way of life. The ideas and practices that follow are merely a starting point for reflection and action. You may already be involved in various forms of community service or sociopolitical activism. You may be exploring ways to make family life richer, to balance work and home life more enjoyably. Anyone endeavoring to raise a healthy child is definitely performing valuable service to the human community. None of us is starting from scratch. I offer the following chapters as nourishment and encouragement for the continuing process of building a truly meaningful life.

Becoming Civilized

❦

In such a huge, complex world, I can't clearly see how I fit in terms of what to contribute or how to be a good citizen. Where do I begin?

If not you, who? If not now, when?

—Hillel

Sir Winston Churchill once showed Mahatma Gandhi the crowning glories of London, and at one point boastfully asked, "Well, Mahatma, what do you think of Western Civilization?" Gandhi wryly replied, "I think it would be a good idea."

Defining our terms and seeing the unadorned truth are always good first steps toward finding a meaningful role to play. The word "civilization" is defined in one dictionary as "advanced stage of social development." Would you say that we are in an advanced stage of social development? We are certainly in an advanced stage of technological development. But wouldn't an advanced stage of social development suggest human beings knowing how to get along with each other, cherishing and sustaining the natural resources of the planet, safeguarding future generations, and generally behaving in a manner that advances the common good? Wouldn't it mean that our children are safer each year on the streets or in the malls, rather than more at risk?

If, like Gandhi, we think Western civilization "would be a good idea," then we must first acknowledge that we have slipped below civilized standards in order to climb back up the ladder to a higher rung. This is both the truth and the challenge: we must simultaneously civilize our own lives and help to civilize a pretty brutal world as well. We may ask, "Will it work?" But the question itself is misleading. It works right now. Instantly. Kind hearts, healthy minds, and a spirit of helpfulness are essential building blocks of any civilization. As we strengthen such qualities in ourselves, they are expressed in everything we do, and our own daily lives become the building blocks of a civilized future for humankind.

Don't overlook the significance of your smallest opportunities for civilized behavior throughout each day. The future has no bigger moments than we experience right now. The world changes for the better with every act of kindness, and for the worse with every act of cruelty. The future is nothing grander than the very next moment, and it arises solely from the present. Where else could it come from?

Being overwhelmed by the nature or scope of the world's problems does not help, though it is easily understandable. Before the modern age, before jet travel and worldwide news reports, before telephones and the Internet, most human beings lived their whole lives in one community and didn't have a great deal of continual information about what was happening everywhere else.

A lifestyle of good works in those days was a pretty

straightforward endeavor, and you could see the difference you made pretty clearly. If you fed the hungry, you would see them gain weight day by day; if you taught skills to the unemployed, you would see them gain employment and get on with their lives. If you took a beggar into your home, you would see one fewer beggar the next day at that same street corner.

In today's world, the faces of the poor shift and change every day. There seem to be an endless number of homeless, unemployed, unskilled, abandoned, addicted, deranged, luckless human beings whose problems far exceed whatever fleeting help we may be able to offer them. We turn on the evening news and are reminded of countless other problems across the globe that seem unbelievably horrendous and far beyond our ability to change. It is easy for us to feel that our acts of civilized behavior and service are essentially meaningless and therefore unnecessary. "What good can I do?" "What difference would it make?" "It would just be to make myself feel better!" "The problems are beyond repair." "I'll give an annual donation to the United Way."

You may even have contacted charitable agencies to inquire about volunteering, and their response (or lack of one) may have deepened your suspicion that your offer to help was of no value. Many nonprofit organizations are terrible about returning phone calls or responding to requests for information. Some may make you feel they are interested only in your wallet. Tunnel vision for their mission may make them unappreciative of your potential for helping out.

But it is not true that you are unneeded. It is not true that your compassionate service is a waste of time or a mere feel-good tactic for yourself. Regardless of how much or how little you may see of the fruits of your efforts, there is a process, a relationship between you and the people you are helping, between you and life itself, which exemplifies the very best of human nature and civilized values. It's another example of process versus object. When we come together to address a certain problem, we experience a process of compassion, friendship, gratitude; we touch each other's hearts and souls.

When we feed even one hungry person with proper respect and affection, that relationship itself is the Kingdom of Heaven right here and now. The point, as Gandhi often made about his struggle to free India from the British Empire, is not to solve all the world's problems, but to dedicate our lives to the effort.

Whether we want such an obligation or not, we do help to create or destroy civilization every day. For the past few hundred years we have been fascinated with machines and technology, so that is the flavor of our civilization. It is an incredible success technologically, far beyond the wildest dreams of our ancestors who started down that path. As Jesus said, "Where your treasure is, there will your heart be also." We have clearly treasured the high-tech side of life more than the human side, so we have created a civilization in which we can phone a friend from 35,000 feet up in an airplane yet need to worry about whether our children may be slain by classmates in school. This is ultimately a question of our priorities—not just national ones but personal ones as well.

The bad news is that if our humanity does not soon catch up with our technology, we will amount to no more than a curious footnote in future history books about a civilization that reached dizzying heights of gadgetry and then seemed to go mad before destroying itself. The good news is that we have the power to reassess our priorities and steer civilization in a direction that makes more sense to us.

What is required is personal commitment, along with practice.

A Practice: CIVILIZING YOUR WORLD

With notepad in hand, spend an hour or so reflecting on how you would like to civilize your world on three levels: (1) your own lifestyle, (2) your immediate community, and (3) a global problem or need.

1. *Civilizing your own lifestyle.*
   To stimulate your thinking in this area, I'll give you examples from my own life of what I mean by this:

   • It feels uncivilized to me to begin or end the day without at least a brief time of prayer and meditation, reminding myself of my biggest priorities.
   • It feels uncivilized to leave a store without having noticed what the clerk looked like and without exchanging genuine regards with him or her.
   • It feels uncivilized to be rude to telephone solicitors. (I never buy anything over the telephone, but I wish them better luck on their next call, or sometimes I try to convince them to get a better job.)
   • Littering feels uncivilized, and so does throwing away plastic bags rather than reusing them.
   • Making a joke or sport out of killing anything—even fleas, ticks, or mosquitoes—feels uncivilized. Likewise, getting angry at an inanimate object like a malfunctioning computer or a flat tire, feels uncivilized.

- It feels uncivilized not to take reasonable care of body, mind, and spirit. For me, that means daily yoga, walking, reading, and meditation.
- It feels uncivilized to read or watch television while I eat a meal.

These are just a few examples. Review your own lifestyle and jot down a few specific "civilizing practices" that you will abide by for at least one month. Don't be afraid to be creative or to do something that might be a little awkward at first. For example, you can ask the names of all the cashiers you deal with that month (or read their name tags), and tell them it's nice to meet them. Just make sure you mean it. If they look at you like you're a weirdo, just explain that it's actually a practice you are doing in order to be a better person. You may be surprised by how much friendliness you uncork.

2. *Civilizing your immediate community.*

- You could reduce the time and money you spend on television, video games, and movies, and decide to spend the same amount of time and money in service to your community instead. Maybe your whole family might take this plunge together. Most communities have many volunteer opportunities, which may be coordinated through a local library, a volunteer coordinating agency, or an interfaith council of local churches.
- Jot down a realistic slice of time that you intend to spend in service work each week for at least a month.
- Most of us have very full plates. Don't sabotage your service commitment by adding a new menu item with-

out removing an existing one. Remember, if you try to do everything, you will probably not do anything very well.

- Find out what's going on in your community and see what draws your interest.

As director of a nonprofit organization myself, I can tell you that the most helpful volunteers are the ones who say, "I'd like to help out x hours per week for a month or so, and then possibly make a long-term commitment if it seems a good fit." That's both honest and promising. A volunteer who says, "I'd be happy to help every now and then, but I can't be tied into a regular schedule or a certain number of hours" is not very much help.

3. *Tackling a global problem or need.*

- Obviously, sending a regular donation to one or more trustworthy charities is a simple and direct way to address problems outside your own community. Again, consistency and commitment, even if the amounts are small, are the most helpful ways to enable a charity to plan its annual budget. If my own organization received even $10 per year from everyone on our mailing list, that would amount to $400,000, which would fully double our current level of operations.
- But there are other exciting ways to engage in global service work too. You could decide to spend some personal time or family vacation time on what is now called a volunteer vacation, in which you (or your whole family) would travel somewhere to participate in a special charitable project.
- The University of Chicago Press publishes a book by

Bill McMillon called *Volunteer Vacations,* which lists hundreds of organizations that need short-term volunteers. Another great source of information is Volunteers for Peace in Belmont, Vermont, a group that publishes an annual directory of hundreds of work camps all over the globe.

• Most cities in America, and a growing number around the world, have local chapters of Habitat for Humanity, a wonderful organization that builds homes for the poor. Habitat relies almost entirely on volunteer labor. Depending on the ages of your children, it could be a wonderful family involvement in your own community, or it could be an unforgettable far-flung experience. One friend of mine who has three young children has been so inspired by his local Habitat experiences that he's now considering a three-year stint in one of Habitat's international projects, where he and his family would live and work at a Habitat site in Africa. What an extraordinary opportunity for those kids! Imagine the skills they'll learn, the values they'll develop, their cultural breadth and wealth of experience by the time they return home. Now that's education!

I have compiled a list of these and other resources, beginning on page 277, to help you find out more about some terrific opportunities to engage in truly civilized service work. Investigating them will lead to many other exciting possibilities as well.

Chicken Little Was Right

I can't help shake this feeling that we're worse off than we've ever been in history. I feel a sense of urgency about helping prevent the complete collapse of decent civilization, no less making the world a better place for my children. Am I imagining this? What can I do?

I do not think you are imagining things. Forget the future for a moment—the decency of our civilization has already collapsed in many ways. It has already become acceptable for our political leaders to be known as liars, cheats, and lechers. We have already accepted not just one or two, but dozens of murders of schoolchildren by their classmates. We have already responded by drafting new laws allowing us to punish small children as if they were adults. We have already accepted ozone reports and air-quality warnings as a fact of life, being frisked at airports, screaming at strangers who cut in front of us on the highway, stepping over mentally ill homeless people on our way to the opera. If a psychic or prophet had revealed these images to us even fifty years ago, we would have said, "Oh no, we will never accept all that."

In a way, it is a cop-out to worry about the complete collapse of civilization in the future rather than to acknowledge and deal with the partial collapse of civilization right now. You and I have plenty of power today to restore decency in the world. If we are concerned about the future, we must give today all our attention and energy. The deep, wonderful secrets of life, the mysterious presence of the Divine, the joy of cherishing each other, the beauty of nature, the satisfaction of helping out—all exist right here, today, in our everyday life. There is no bigger ball field on which to find meaning. The future is no more worthwhile to save than the present. Can we have fun in the future? No. The present is the only time we can really enjoy living.

We can start by asking ourselves some obvious questions: Is the dominant consumption-obsessed lifestyle what you believe in? Is it what you believe life is primarily about? If so, fine. Devote all your time to it, as most people are doing. But if you believe life is also about something deeper, then how much energy are you spending toward that deeper reality?

The basics of a decent, civilized life are timeless: get up in the morning, take reasonable care of your body, mind, and soul; do some kind of work that benefits the world instead of harms it; respect and cherish other people; and then get some sleep. It's important to keep your big view deep but simple, and to pass such a view on to your kids. They desperately need a bigger view than television, malls, and the salaries of their favorite athletes and movie stars.

Without wholesome, happy, functional children, there is no optimistic future for civilization. If we want to understand why the sky is falling, we need to ask ourselves why life seems to be of so little joy and value to our kids. I discussed some of those issues in a preceding chapter, focusing mostly on our views of child-raising. But we also need to look at the largest possible picture as well.

In my opinion, one sentence can sum up the whole

thing—not only our own and our kids' problems, but our planetary problems too, from pollution to wars:

Human life is very deep, and our dominant modern lifestyle is not.

We've progressed so much technologically in the past couple hundred years that we have understandably gotten caught up in the details, the support systems, the trivia, and have lost the core of simple joy that makes it all worthwhile.

Right now, while you are reading this, take a moment to center yourself in your body, in this place you sit; feel yourself breathing, and smile. Don't just speed-read on to the next paragraph, please. Let go of past and future. Appreciate that you're alive; appreciate knowing how to read. Appreciate knowing about spiritual wisdom. Bring a soft smile of gratitude into your heart and onto your face.

This is what we rarely pass on to our kids. Our kids don't get the message from us that being alive feels good. We may say it to them occasionally, but how do we show it in our everyday activities? Even the best, most loving adults often seem to be working themselves into the ground, keeping up a frantic pace just to pay the bills and to keep resolving each day's repairs, breakdowns, details, and little crises.

There is a great line in the old movie *When Harry Met Sally* that can be a useful reminder to us all. In one scene, Meg Ryan is in a restaurant with Billy Crystal. She's trying to prove how easily men can be fooled by women who fake orgasm, so she does a very convincing job of going into orgasmic ecstasy over her french fries. She really gets into it, and attracts a lot of attention. The waitress then goes to the older woman at the next table and says, "Can I take your order?" and the woman says excitedly, "I'll have whatever she's having!"

If there was an invisible child or teenager attached to your hip, following you throughout the day, would he see somebody who is really enjoying the moments of who you are and what you're doing? Would he see somebody who would inspire him to say, "I want what she's having," or "I can't wait to be a grown-up?" Would he see peace? Would he see a depth of joy and contentment, equanimity, a gracefulness about life?

How many simple, peaceful, truly happy adults do our kids get to see? How many of us are deeply content with our lives and enjoy what we do? How many of us are relaxed about getting older and unafraid of dying? How many of us are happy and calm, with time to play hooky from work every now and then in order to spend some unplanned, unstructured, unproductive time with our families?

No wonder so many kids are suicidal, homicidal, and drug-addicted. They're getting a strong message that we adults have very few choices of how we can spend our time. People work fifty-, sixty-, seventy-hour weeks for a ten-day or two-week vacation a year. Many of us loudly lament how much we dislike our jobs, or what a grind it is to earn a decent living. You must admit, from a kid's point of view, growing up may not look very appealing.

Think about it: "Honey, I'd love to coach your soccer team this year, but I just can't. I'm sorry. I have to do such-and-such. I wish I didn't have to, but I do." How many times do our kids hear such stuff? "I can't, I can't, I can't." "I have to, I have to, I have to." Besides seeing so many joyless or downright angry adults in schools, businesses, and government, kids must also get the impression that being an adult means being powerless. Does this inspire young people to take good care of themselves? Teen smoking is actually on the rise. Many teens exist almost entirely on junk food. Yet they know better than any generation before them that these choices are linked to reduced quality of life and even premature death. They do not seem to care. When life looks joyless and meaningless, why try to prolong it?

Many people have never asked themselves the question, "What do I most deeply believe in?" One day has just gone into the next. You follow a career in which you can make a lot of money or a field in which you have some talent. That's too easy. What are your deepest values as a human being? What do you really believe in? Time to get back to the basics.

A Practice: VALUES EXERCISE

If you had to write an essay called "My Values as a Human Being," could you? Spend an evening or a day or even a weekend sometime, as a personal retreat, to write down your values. Prisoners I work with, for example, may write, "I don't believe in stealing. I want to be honest. I want to be trustworthy." Then they get a chance to see whether their behavior matches their values.

However you write out your values, try to keep them simple and brief. Don't go into long preachments about why you feel the way you do, or how others should feel or respond. This exercise is for you. You do not need to justify your values or create a perfect world, merely to write some essential things you feel about what it takes to be a good human being.

You may want to separate your writing and reviewing by a few hours or even several days. When you do review what you have written, look it over with cold, hard truth. Ask yourself:

- Do I abide by these values?
- Do I embody them? Can others clearly see my values in word and deed?
- How do I prioritize my time in relation to my deepest values? For example, if you have a deep love for nature, how much time do you spend in it? How many sunsets do you watch? How long has it been since you've camped out overnight? You're not going to live forever. If you believe that a family mealtime is a wonderful thing, how often are your family's breakfasts and dinners calm, relaxed, happy get-togethers during which you really get to share your lives with each other? If not, why not? Shouldn't deep values receive high priority even if it means making some major changes?
- Framing one's values is a good exercise. Living up to them is the challenge. Am I willing to live more as I believe instead of rationalizing somehow that life has me pinned in a corner? In order to live deeply and deliberately, in order to develop a good life, we need to take the time to ask ourselves deep questions. If we do not choose to take the time, our children may not choose to take the time when they are adults; and their children and their children—and then you see why civilization is going downhill.

We can indeed stop the sky from falling, but it's going to cost us some time. Our time could not possibly be better spent, even if that means trimming down our lifestyle so that one parent can quit working in order to home-school the children. With public schools being such a mess, home-schooling networks are springing up all over the place, and most participants find them to be tremendously empowering and sheer fun as well. No matter how hard the changes or the challenge, I find no one ever regretting taking big steps to live more in tune with their deepest values.

The Big Activism

You hear this phrase "simple living" all the time these days. I'm never really sure what it refers to. If it means living like a monk or saving rubber bands or buying only used clothing, I can't relate. How can I begin to live more simply in a realistic way?

The most valuable form of world-changing activism in this day and age may be to explore a lifestyle based on simple living and simple joy. It may take toning down our materialistic demands and figuring out how to live on less income. But that process itself would begin to save some of the world's resources and thereby address many of the world's pressing problems, as well as give us more time with our families and communities.

One of the most fascinating mysteries of human behavior is the process by which we enslave ourselves with golden chains. We think we are fortunate when we can satisfy our desires, but by the time we blink our eyes, those desires have become needs. Something that was once optional has all by itself become essential. It no longer brings us the same delight it once did, yet we live in fear of losing it.

We amass so many "labor-saving" devices that we're working sixty-hour-a-week jobs to support them all. Have they saved us labor yet? Not if we can no longer do without them. Gadgets as trivial as trash compactors or icemakers have insinuated themselves very deeply into our emotional structure. It's really a very strange phenomenon.

Take automobiles, for example. The first ads for cars appealed to the country-club set. But within a short time, houses and shopping centers, schools and factories, and government offices were designed and located on the basis of automobile travel. Those who chose not to own or ride in motor vehicles were essentially penalized and forced to keep up with the times. How many people today can abstain from traveling in cars?

Multiply that example by thousands of "optional" inventions, from Henry Ford's time to our age of e-mail and cellular phones. Millions of people, young and old—precious, divine vehicles of God—are rushing to enslave themselves to banks and other corporations for the rest of their lives, to support a complex and burdensome lifestyle that has little to do with joy or truth or freedom. The credit card companies are offering free poisoned cake, and we are feasting on it by the truckful, losing more peace of mind by the day. Have we gone nuts?

There is certainly an alternative to being consumer sheep fattened for the slaughter. We can create a simpler lifestyle, which not only requires a lot less money but also gives us more time for the things that really do matter. We can go from "loving things and using people" to "loving people and using things."

Many people have said to me, "Oh, I could easily live in a simpler way or dedicate my life to a cause I believe in, but it would be unfair to my children. What about health care? What about their college education? I don't feel I have the right to limit their opportunities." A Hasidic story retold by Rabbi Benjamin Twerski speaks beautifully to this point:

THE ULTIMATE CHILD

"Oh where is that ultimate child?" cried the Rabbi of Pscizche. "Where is that child who is driving the entire world insane?"

Once in his youth, the Rabbi confronted a man who was totally immersed in his business ventures. "Why are you so totally absorbed in trying to make money? Why do you not devote time to prayer and Torah study?" The man responded, "You see, Rabbi, I really do not require that much to live on, but I must work to provide for my family, especially my *child* and his future."

Years went by and that child became a grown man. He, too, became engrossed in pursuit of worldly assets. "Why do you not take time out to further your spiritual growth? The Rabbi of Pscizche asked of him. The man answered, "I cannot, Rabbi. For though I do not need much for myself, I must think of my *child,* and his future."

Then that child grows up, and the story is again the same. It repeats itself generation after generation. No one has adequate time to live according to his beliefs because everyone must provide for *his* child, and so on.

"Somewhere, then," the Rabbi exclaimed, "perhaps at the end of time, we will find that ultimate child, for whose welfare countless generations have so toiled that they've neglected their own values in the process. Where, where is that

ultimate child? Is he not but a fiction? A non-
existent end-point? An illusion that has driven
the entire world into an insane striving toward
futility?"

Our children have the same needs we do: to live joyfully
and meaningfully. As we can see all around us, no amount
of privilege or affluence guarantees that. The way to give
our children the maximum chance for a joyful and meaningful life is to be living one *with* them, not sacrificing ours
for theirs. Our children's destiny is divinely linked with
ours. If it is our calling to work with the poor, or to com-
pose music, or to build houses, these are not irrelevant factors in our children's lives. If we feel drawn to live more
simply, we can share that "experiment in truth," to use
Gandhi's term, with our children. This is what makes them
different from someone else's children.

No matter how we live, we define the boundaries of our
children's experience to some degree, and this is the way it
is supposed to be. Our personal interests and values necessarily define much about our children's lives, so we must
make sure we pass on deliberate and deep values, and embody them ourselves.

We are all working pretty hard these days. Many of us may
think we can't get by on less. But I recently looked around
a typical suburban neighborhood of twenty houses, and I
realized there were probably twenty lawn mowers, ten
chainsaws, fifteen Weed Eaters and a lot of other expensive
contraptions, which each family may only use a few days a
year. Among those twenty houses I counted about forty-
five cars, costing a fortune in insurance, repair, registration,

gas, and so forth. Those twenty families may own fifty or more televisions and audio systems and God knows how many computer games their small children may not even play anymore. This isn't food and shelter we're talking about. Are we working ourselves into the ground to support a bunch of stuff that mostly sits in the closet or on a shelf?

When I was growing up in the 1950s, only one house on my block had a television. A bunch of us would gather at that neighbor's house to watch something—which, of course, provided natural opportunities to socialize with the neighbors. This still goes on in many other countries. But in our society, TV has become the opposite force: even poor families may have little TVs in several rooms, so we hardly even socialize with our own families, let alone our neighbors.

This is a strong example that more is not always better. In cultures where people must share limited resources— TVs, tools, vehicles—their sense of community is much stronger. We have accepted a model of progress and personal choice that has isolated us as individuals and actually damaged our family and community life a great deal. Is it really progress? These days, it is nothing short of political activism to go against that tide and live more simply. We must think for ourselves and talk with friends and have the guts to try some things differently to take the pressure off. This is a fitting time to explore various old and new ways of living with others in intentional communities, cohousing, collective ownership of vehicles and tools, and other ways to cut down on the wasteful expense of modern living.

Bulk buying, carpooling, exchanging goods and services, even buying an apartment building or piece of land to live on with friends—there are many ways you can save money by teaming up with others. Begin by having open discussions with friends and neighbors about what you all spend money on. Many ways to save will become obvious—all those lawn mowers and so forth I mentioned above which are only used a few hours here and there. Share the table saw and drill press with Ernie down the block. We must overcome our contemporary attitude of not wanting to share and not wanting to depend on each other. It has not worked. We need to need each other, we need to learn to share, just as we learned in kindergarten. This is the heart of modern-day community organizing.

If you don't feel ready for huge steps like co-ownership or slashing your salary in half, take small steps. Make one practical change this week that will allow you to live on a little bit less and be less burdened with possessions. Cut down to one TV in your home (and cut down your use of it greatly.)

Most of the ideas and practices mentioned in this book will enhance a simpler lifestyle: eat meals with your family, go for walks, do daily readings of spiritual stories, occasionally play hooky together, and go skip stones across a pond.

It takes work, of course. Anytime we step aside from the crowds there will be work involved. Mahatma Gandhi called his autobiography *The Story of My Experiment with Truth.* That is the opportunity each of us has. Not just what we read in the evening, not just in church on Sundays, but to make our everyday lives a grand, noble, good-humored experiment in truth—where we live, what we do for a living, how our children are educated, the causes we embrace and support, how we spend our free time. All one thing. An undivided whole. A deliberate life. A rare thing in today's world.

A Practice: LIVING SIMPLY

It can be a bit overwhelming to talk conceptually about simplifying our lives. However, once we take it out of the abstract, we see the process entails nothing more than some straightforward steps toward living more in tune with our beliefs. Here are a few ways to begin:

1. *Get out of debt and stay out!* Pay off your current debts as soon as possible and live within your means. Other than a home or land, if you can't afford to pay in full for something, don't buy it. Never buy anything on credit, even a car. You will discover many good things about yourself if you follow this advice. Your kids will profit greatly. Especially never go into debt for a wedding or graduation, for tuxes, gowns, limos, and so on. This is a horribly misguided way of expressing love. It creates stress and reinforces distorted views about "the good life." Celebrate special affairs with potlucks, picnics, and other happy, community-style events. Let friends and family work together as an expression of their love for the individuals at the heart of the celebration. This is about a lot more than just saving money.

2. *Buy one, give away one.* Get into the habit of giving away one old item for each new item you buy. Want a new CD? Give away—or sell—an old one. Want a new shirt? Shoes? Same thing. Again, your kids will learn a lot from this, and your home will be less cluttered. When you're ready to reduce clutter even more, give *two* away for every one you buy. It is a wonderful feeling not to be

burdened by too many possessions. This practice also helps you and your family think twice before buying!

3. *Quit smoking and drinking!* As of this writing, over sixty million Americans smoke. A pack-a-day smoker these days is spending about $100 per month, or $1,200 per year. Double that amount for two people in the same family, or if you smoke a couple packs a day. Add in a similar amount for beer, wine, or liquor, and you can see that many people who may consider themselves low-income or even poor are working about a quarter of their time to support habits that shorten their lives, weaken their health, and provide a bad example for their children. How much do you spend on smoking and drinking in the course of a year? Are there other ways you can think of to spend that same amount of money that would be more enjoyable for you and your family?

4. *Boycott holiday buying madness forever.* Think about how much of your annual salary you spend on gifts that break and rust and are not even appreciated very long by their recipients. Sita, Josh, and I agreed years ago not to buy gifts for each other on birthdays or holidays. What a relief! And believe it or not, your friends and family will survive the shock if you extend it to them as well. We make plans to be with each other and do something together instead of rushing to the mall to buy meaningless junk. We make something ourselves, or prepare a favorite meal or special dessert. We may go hiking or swimming, or see a movie together. When we do buy a gift for each other, it's not on a special day, it's just something that we know would be perfect for that person, or that we already know is needed. Abandoning holiday and birthday gifts makes those spontaneous gifts very heartfelt on both sides.

5. *Eat more home-cooked meals.* Restaurant food, fast food, and take-out meals from your local markets can add up to a surprising annual cost and, for the most part, are not very nutritional. Brainstorm how you can be a little more resourceful and cut this expense at least in half. Taking your lunch to work, for example, or making and freezing several dinners on a weekend so that you just have to heat them up during the week. Besides the financial side, how do you feel about your food habits? Are you eating the way you believe is best, or is this perhaps one more example of fence-sitting that results in stress? Resolve to be more deliberate about how, what, and when you eat.

These suggestions and practices are not extraordinary sacrifices. They are a form of mild, constructive activism that help us take more charge of our lives and strengthen bonds with our families and communities. Don't let anyone convince you that you are a nut for working with any of these ideas. You truly have nothing to lose but your golden chains.

A House Too Small May Be a Blessing

What about all the material things I love? Isn't it worth it to work hard for what I love, the creature comforts, luxury, fine food and clothing, a beautiful home? Isn't all of that part of a joyful life?

Money and our relationship to it certainly constitute one of the great mysteries of human nature. Having too little money seems to force our minds to dwell on money most of the time. Having too much money seems to create the same effect. And yet, "too little" and "too much" are relative terms; what is too little or too much in one person's eyes may look entirely different in another's. Our attitudes about too little or too much also change as we proceed through various stages of our lives. When I was a kid, I wanted gobs of money. Now I find it tremendous fun not to own anything, and to be paid room and board plus $50 per month. I'm a much happier kid this way. I love my lifestyle. What we can agree on, if we are wise, is that our relationship to money is a challenging issue in life's journey, and is worthy of frank reflection so that our lives can express what we believe in, rather than being in conflict with ourselves. The vast majority of us have at least some degree of conflict over the role of money in our lives, even if we insist that we don't. It's a tricky issue and runs very deep.

To illustrate this point, at a workshop a few years ago in California, I asked a few seemingly random questions of the participants. I pointed toward one woman and asked, "Where were you born?" She replied, "Miami." To another I said, "How tall are you?" He replied, "Five feet ten." I asked a few other innocuous questions, which people easily answered, and then said to one gray-haired, well-dressed gentleman, "What was your gross income last year?"

The fellow first hesitated uncomfortably for several seconds, and then stammered a little, until I took him off the spot. My point was simply that if we are as comfortable with how much money we earn as we are with the color of our eyes or where we live, then the answer to my question would have flowed as effortlessly as all the rest of the answers. Most of us are not entirely comfortable with how much money we earn or spend. In some crowds, we may be uncomfortable because it sounds like too little, and in other crowds, the same amount embarrasses us because it seems like too much. The truth is, we have many voices within ourselves. Let's face it: money is tricky. It merits some attention.

I personally disagree with the "abundance and prosperity" teachings so popular in modern times. The general drift seems to be that we can pursue wealth and wisdom equally; we can indulge all our desires and still be devoted to God; we can have the holdings of Ted Turner with the heart of Mother Teresa.

I find three major problems with those teachings. First, I have read the Old Testament, New Testament, Koran, Mahabharata, Ramayana, Dhammapada, the scriptures of

Baha'ullah, and other sacred texts from many ancient traditions, and I cannot find these "abundance" teachings supported by any of the masters. In several sacred texts, such as the Yoga Vasisth of Hinduism, we come across the idea that if we are born into wealth, or if wealth comes to us incidentally, it is not essential to give it up; we can take responsibility for it and use it wisely as a compassionate citizen or benefactor. But I know of no classic spiritual teaching that encourages us to actively seek wealth if we don't already have it. Quite the contrary, there are countless references to the folly or dangers of doing so.

> Whoever loves money, never has money enough; whoever loves wealth is never satisfied with his income.
>
> —Ecclesiastes 5:10

The second problem I have with the modern exhortations to get rich is that you can almost smell the underlying fear in those writings, workshops, and seminars—bright, shining, transcendent beings feeling small and needful, repeating demeaning affirmations about wealth, posting photos of luxury cars on their refrigerators to "attract" such objects into their lives. I love who we truly are, so this is very sad to me. It is like seeing the king's own children behaving like poor orphans who must beg and bow down to graven images in order to get alms. It hurts to see.

Third, the prosperity bandwagon also smacks of an extreme resistance to experience the grand adventure of life, which will almost certainly take us through periods of adversity as well as prosperity. We can do adversity! It's part of the fun! Would you go to see a Star Wars movie if it guaranteed no danger, no setbacks, no cliffhangers? Life is a far greater adventure than a movie, and we know from the start that we're all going to get sick, we're all going to age, die, and lose everything tangible. Great! Now that we've accepted that, we can be good sports about the whole roller-coaster ride, and do it with gusto. Like Ram Dass used to say, "Grab tightly, let go lightly." Be fully involved, but not resistant to loss and change.

One of the great ironies of our particular age is that most of us do not feel wealthy even though we take for granted a level of comfort and luxury unparalleled in world history. What has gotten so out of whack in modern times? Why does it require so much income merely to pay the bills? Most of us are working much too hard. Why?

Maybe it's because consumerism encourages us from the time we're born to have ceaseless desires. To put it simply, we want so much, all the time, that we have not even noticed how much quality of life we give up in the process of buying, comparing, repairing, safeguarding, discarding, and replacing. Our lives run us instead of us running our lives. There's no way around the fact that we can't have everything. Our own experience tells us we can't have a lot of time *and* a lot of possessions. Jesus tells us we can't have God and Mammon. Folk wisdom tells us we can't have our cake and eat it too. Something has to give. But it can be given joyfully. Most of us would like more time, so we need to reduce our financial needs. No way around it. But we can decide to love the old car that's paid for; to enjoy the old sofa from the thrift shop; to appreciate simple, home-cooked meals.

If we see clearly what our conflicts are, then we can be deliberate about the resulting choices we make. The peace so many of us seek is no more than the removal of all these conflicts and divisions and levels of frustration and denial. We are at peace when our lives become one undivided whole—not perfect, but deliberate. No internal wars sapping our energy. Whether it's cars or clothes or furniture, we can strengthen our inner dignity so that we are no longer slaves to fashion. We can rethink our basic values and help our kids form a deeper sense of self-worth than the cost of the clothes they wear. When we simplify, we wind up with unexpected benefits such as spending more time together, because we live in a smaller house than before, or because we share one TV rather than everyone having their own. It may benefit our children for their whole lives if they share a room growing up rather than having the luxury of having their own. I went to a Toys "Я" Us store once with a wealthy Hollywood producer who bought two easels, two sets of paints, two slides, and other double items for her twin three-year-olds because she didn't want them to quarrel over their toys. Will that really benefit them in the long run?

A Practice: SACRED READING

How are we supposed to remember this uncommon perspective of simple living and family and community cooperation when, from the time we set foot outside our door each morning, we find ourselves besieged by messages of *buy, get, have, bigger, better, more?* How do we expect our children to keep a balanced perspective when they too are besieged by such messages everywhere they go?

One of the most enjoyable ways of keeping the larger perspectives in our minds is the daily morning practice of sacred readings, books that were written hundreds or thousands of years before our era, or contemporary books that point us to the same ageless principles.

To dip a toe into timeless waters even for a few minutes each morning can broaden our perspectives immensely over a period of time. It helps us to see and to live in a larger dimension than the tiny little slice of time and one specific culture we find ourselves in. When we can remember the bigger picture, it is a lot easier to find our way through the smaller one.

1. *With a group:*

- In a family or community, set time aside for daily readings. Mornings usually work best, before family or community members split off for the day. Sita and I would do our silent meditation, and then wake Josh for the reading, so it was the very first activity of his day from the time he was three or four years old until he left home at eighteen. He would snuggle with Sita while I read. Sometimes he would be sleepy, sometimes fully engrossed, but we had faith that even if he did not understand every word of the reading, he was still accumulating something day after day. Sure enough, by the time he was an adolescent, he had a very good basic idea of the flavor of the world's great religions.
- The reading does not have to be long or heavy. Some classic children's stories are wonderful for the whole

family, such as C. S. Lewis's *Chronicles of Narnia,* which Seedsowers Press called "one of the ten most important Christian books in the last two hundred years." And some adult stories, like the William Buck version of the Hindu classic, *Ramayana,* are lively and entertaining enough for children to enjoy. (See pages 268–276 for a list of some others of my family's favorite sacred readings books.)

• In our community, Kindness House, we take turns reading, giving each person at least a week at a time so he or she has the chance to choose longer readings and break them up over several days. Stories are usually more enjoyable to read aloud than straight scripture or didactic teachings, and most good spiritual stories appeal to all ages.

2. *By yourself:*

• It's really the same practice, except you'll be reading to yourself, and not necessarily aloud (although it's sometimes effective to read aloud even when you are alone; I recommend it). Alone, you'll have the luxury of going as slowly as you like, taking time for the reading to sink in.

• Even if you can't do daily readings together with your friends or family, you can still do this practice long-distance with loved ones in other places. After Josh left home, he continued to read from the Ramayana and so did we, and we would discuss it in phone calls and letters. Hanging out with the same holy book is a wonderful way to maintain a deep connection with loved ones.

3. *A few tips:*

- Because our attention span has been under assault since the invention of television, we may not be in the habit of reading very slowly or reflectively. With this practice, remember that quantity is not the goal. Classic spiritual stories, especially, are meant to be studied over and over again for a whole lifetime. As we deepen through our practices, we gain more fun from the same teachings each time through.

- Don't assume that your reading must hit you over the head with a blatant moral or message. Our daily life has countless subtleties, and so do holy readings. Children especially do not have to be told what it all "means." Let them hear whatever they can hear. Have faith that all powerful spiritual readings have many levels of meaning.

- It is very useful to tap into a variety of ancient wisdom, rather than from just one tradition. It is illuminating to realize that life's most pressing concerns and personal challenges do not change from culture to culture.

- Most ancient holy books are written in language that by today's standards sometimes comes across as sexist or racist or terribly outdated. While I often wince as I meet such passages, I know in my heart that the great ancient teachings still hold tremendous value to us underneath that old language. We can gain a lot by learning to grin and bear those turns of phrase and look deeper for the real gold hidden beneath the mud. Sacred stories have tremendous power even if they were imperfectly set down in words. It is part of our spiritual work to wrestle with passages that bother us rather than toss the teachings aside as outdated or politically incorrect, concluding that we have nothing to learn from them. Such soul-searching has always been a significant part of the spiritual journey.

What Are We Thinking?

———————— 🍃 ————————

I'm not happy about a lot of the things that my kids watch, listen to, and read, but what am I supposed to do—censor them? Do my kids need to be sheltered from reality in order to have a good life?

> *Blow up your TV,*
> *Throw away your paper,*
> *Move to the country,*
> *Build you a home.*
> *Plant a little garden,*
> *Eat a lot of peaches,*
> *Try to find Jesus*
> *On your own.*
>
> —John Prine, "Spanish Pipe Dream"

In the mid-1970s, I was invited to speak at the summer solstice gathering of the American Sikh organization called 3HO (Happy, Healthy, Holy Organization). Over a thousand white-robed, turban-clad, extremely self-disciplined young men and women sat on the ground in nearly 120-degree New Mexico heat. These were serious spiritual seekers, no doubt about it. Their leader, Yogi Bhajan, spoke in a thundering voice: "How many of you have eaten meat during the past year?" Not a single person raised his or her hand. He continued, "How many of you have had alcohol or drugs?" Again, not a hand was raised. Looks of self-satisfaction and pride filled the grounds.

Then he dropped the bomb: "How many of you have seen *The Exorcist?*" The classic horror film, pretty lame by today's standards, had been released just a few months earlier.

Several hundred hands slowly, sheepishly went up, and Yogi Bhajan shook his head back and forth as if in disgust. He finally said, "You are so careful over what you put into your body, and you care nothing at all about what you put into your mind."

So careful not only of what we put into our bodies, but also of how we look, how we physically feel. Consider how much we fuss over our cholesterol levels or blood pressure or whether we have selected precisely the right shoes for walking, running, hiking. What about our minds? Is there no such thing as pollution of the mind? Feeding toxins to the mind? Stagnation of the mind? At that meeting many years ago, Yogi Bhajan went on to admonish his flock for their combination of ignorance and arrogance regarding the proper care and maintenance of such an extraordinary gift as the human mind. He told them it is a precious thing; it is not to be abused or misused.

You and I and everyone else may have a wide range of criteria for what constitutes abuse or misuse of the mind, but common sense tells us that it is probably not proper care and use of the mind to watch four hours of commercial television per day, which is the average of American children.

Common sense tells us it is probably not a great idea for any of us, especially children, to watch movies that depict human beings killing and maiming and hating and brutalizing others. Nor to listen to music about committing suicide or murdering cops or just hating life in general. This is not a matter of censoring out reality, unless you feel that to abstain from heroin or crack is censoring out reality as well. We "censor" things out of our experience constantly, because we feel one thing or another is not good for us. Yet, as Yogi Bhajan pointed out, when push comes to shove, look how little we respect our minds and the minds of our children. What are we thinking? That we can expose our minds to anything and not be influenced by it? A single freeze-frame memory can haunt the mind until our dying day.

I testified once in the death-penalty phase of a young man's murder trial. The prosecutor had several huge color posters of this young man's victim from photos taken before her body was moved. I will not describe to you what she looked like in those photos, nor the position she was in, nor what her injuries were, because I want to spare your mind from those images. I will just say two things about that experience:

1. Although I am a seasoned criminal justice professional, those photos left permanent, disturbing impressions in my mind.
2. Those photos were no worse than some of the gory special effects your kids have access to when they go to the movies or rent "slasher" videos. If you think they leave no lingering effects, you have not been reading the newspapers about the increase in violent youth crimes.

In his sobering book *On Killing,* Lieutenant Colonel David Grossman, a retired Army Ranger and psychologist specializing in the effects on children of television and video games, points out that the Air Force uses flight simulators to turn ordinary young men and women into pilots. The Army uses war simulators to help young soldiers overcome their instinctive reluctance to kill. Dr. Grossman says that many of the new video games could accurately be seen as "sociopath simulators," working very effectively to turn children and adolescents into murderous sociopaths, cackling with glee and making wisecracks as they kill innocent people and stray animals.

Dr. Grossman emphasizes that video games are very different from the age-old "Bang bang; you're dead" sort of play that children—and even tiger cubs, kittens, bear cubs, foxes—engage in. When playing video games, children develop motor responses to kill without any repercussions or checks and balances that a playmate would naturally provide. One game's worth of killing may include thousands of dead bad guys, good guys, innocent bystanders—all in the "fun" of the game. Dr. Grossman, a dedicated military man, maintains that "violent video games are the equivalent of putting an assault rifle in the hands of every child in America." Do our children come pre-equipped morally and philosophically and emotionally to own an assault rifle of their very own?

It is indeed proper to censor not only our children's viewing and listening but also our own. We don't have to get puritanical or humorless about it, just a little more respectful of the mind as a precious instrument that we need to care for a little better. The problems do not just revolve around violent images but, in the case of television, around the speed of images as well. Researchers have begun to link a host of learning disabilities—attention deficit disorder, hyperactivity, even dyslexia—with actual neurological changes in the brain from too much television.

Even award-winning children's television shows like *Sesame Street* often feature frenetically paced sequences which the producers feel are necessary to sustain the attention of a sophisticated modern child. The only enduring bastion of calmness and deep respect for children as people seems to be *Mr. Rogers' Neighborhood*. I am happy to call Fred Rogers a dear friend, and I know there is great depth and love for children behind his slow, deliberate style of speaking, and taking time on-camera to change his shoes and sweater. Mr. Rogers may be about the only calm, soft-spoken adult many of our children ever get to see on television.

If you and I wish to limit some of our children's exposure to television, movies, and music, yet expose our own minds to anything and everything that beckons us, it is absolutely true that they will resent us and probably sneak behind our backs to see or hear whatever they want. But if you and I are genuinely involved in cleaning up the theater of our own minds as well, then our children are far less likely to resent us or sneak behind our backs, even if they grumble a little.

The main question is, Do we or do we not believe that the mind merits a reasonable degree of protection from graphic images or lyrics that usually have more to do with making a buck than with anything worthwhile or noble? Besides violence and brain-altering speediness, television presents countless shows that portray the shallowest, crassest, most self-centered values imaginable, punctuated by commercials that entice viewers to make those superficial values their own.

We did not own a television when Josh was very young. When he was about five years old we lost him to my brother's house, where he could be found sitting mesmerized in front of soaps, game shows, commercials—anything at all. We realized the cat was out of the bag, and we could no longer avoid dealing with the question of television in our home. So we struck a compromise: we would get a TV, but there would be ground rules. The first one was that Josh would no longer go to my brother's home to watch television. The rest of the ground rules are reconstructed in the following practice, and I can tell you that they worked beautifully for the next thirteen years.

We also had one more, actually: we only watched TV *together*. Over the years, that turned out to be about two hours a week of television, usually including about two sitcoms and a drama show. Sita and I had to admit that it was thoroughly enjoyable. The whole family moved from the *Mary Tyler Moore Show* and *Six Million Dollar Man* years, through the *Taxi* and *Hill Street Blues* years, the *Cheers* and *L.A. Law* years. We watched historic miniseries like *Roots* and *Jesus of Nazareth*. Josh never really fought against our ground rules and, in fact, appreciated not wasting a lot of his childhood zoned out in front of a flickering screen. The shows weren't perfect, but they were fun, and they weren't without some value. Josh especially loved good sitcoms, the ones with heart and humanity. *Cheers* was a family favorite, and as life would have it, his very first acting job after moving out to Los Angeles was as the waitress Carla's son, Gino, on *Cheers*. He appeared prominently in four episodes and had a whale of a time. I mention this because I want to make it clear that my family and I are absolutely not television haters. We have had a lot of fun with our relationship to television, and at the same time recognize the need for serious boundaries because it is such a powerful influence in our lives and our children's.

A Practice: A TELEVISION VOW

1. I will not turn the TV on unless I know what I'm going to watch.
2. I will not watch shows that primarily exploit the viewers' fascination with sex, violence, power, and wealth. (There goes the evening news!)
3. I will not keep the television on after my intended programs are over.
4. I will mute my television as soon as it goes to a commercial (and not watch the commercial either, except to glance occasionally to see when the show comes back on.)
5. I will not talk on the phone or try to accomplish other things with the TV on in the background.
6. My family will choose at least one full day each week as a "television-free day" for our entire household.

Such a simple view can be the beginning of a new deliberateness in your life which you may then decide to extend to the movies you see, the videos you rent, the books and magazines you read, and even the products you buy. It can begin to give you a little freedom from exploitation, and some brief quiet spaces during which joy can arise from within.

Try to get your children to take the same vow. Whether you realize it or not, television shows and commercials deposit an enormous number of influences and associations into our brains, even (or especially) into the brains of infants and toddlers who seem not to notice. Like Yogi Bhajan's disciples, do you spend much more energy guarding what goes into your children's bodies than what goes into their minds? Have you watched their shows with them to see what you think?

If you do this practice for a month or two, you will probably discover that you have more fun with your family, that you all choose your programs more thoughtfully, and that without commercials you enjoy those shows more. Be a little more respectful of what you expose your mind and heart to, and see what comes of it.

The Gospel of Following Bliss

How do art and work and service fit together? What if I love being a poet or a dancer? Is that too selfish? Can I pursue my passion and still help the world?

In the Hindu scriptures, Lord Krishna says, "Better to do your own *dharma* [path, duty], even if it seems devoid of merit, than to imitate someone else's *dharma* which may seem more worthwhile." At first, especially to a modern American or other Westerner, Krishna's counsel may seem to reinforce our individualistic outlook, which says, "Do whatever you need or want to do, follow your own dreams, and don't consider anyone else." But when Krishna says, basically, "Do your own thing," he means the opposite of what most of us mean when we say the very same words. He is always speaking from an assumption of sacred duty toward the common good; he's just pointing out that we all have different roles to play in that common good. Different roles, but make no mistake about it, the same mission: To live in a way that benefits rather than harms; to live in a way, however humble or exalted, that glorifies and uplifts creation.

Obviously, all the arts fit into the grand scheme of uplifting creation, as does selling shoes or driving a cab or any other honorable calling. Therefore, the proper question is not "What role should I play?" but "How should I play my role?" A streetsweeper or prime minister, a dancer or doctor, may or may not see the world through the eyes of uplifting creation, of contributing to the common good. To the degree we do, the world is enriched by the parts we play. To the degree we do not, our parts may be, to quote Shakespeare, "full of sound and fury, signifying nothing."

All of us have instincts for a self-centered life, and we also have instincts for true community. And we have free will to choose between them. In the view of the classic wisdom traditions, it is essential to dedicate our lives to the good. An undedicated life is filled with anxieties and headaches, unfulfilled ambitions and regrets. A conscious choice to dedicate our lives to the good—which in Christian terminology is none other than the "decision for Christ"—is independent of our unique callings, passions, talents, bliss, ambitions, and so forth. It's first and foremost a choice of what sort of person to be, no matter whether we drive an oxcart or a Ferrari, live in a cave or a penthouse, inhabit the first century or the twenty-first.

Once we decide what sort of person we will be, then our talents or callings come into the picture as the means by which we express our goodness to the world. Next the question arises: How do we know what our unique path, our dharma, is? In the Bhagavad Gita, Krishna tells Arjun that he is the speed in a horse's legs, the light in the sun, the wetness in water, the fragrance in flowers, and without doubt he is the passion in your heart for art and in mine for music, the business acumen in one person's mind, the persistence in another's for wiping out hunger, and in yet another's he shines forth as brilliance in quantum physics.

He is the playwright and the player and the play and the audience.

Every other religion, as well, reminds us that we are all intentional elements of God's creation and we were put here for a purpose in keeping with our talents, energy, and circumstances. I have a dear friend who was born into a terrible situation—unwanted, neglected, even tortured by her own mother. She became a midwife, to give other newborns a better start than she had. With great commitment and deep affection, she has ushered many babies into this world. If not for her own horrible birth, this fulfilling career may never have occurred to her.

My son, Josh, had a natural passion for acting since he was six or seven years old. To suppress that would be to forget that God had instilled it in him. So we helped him "follow his bliss," as Joseph Campbell put it, at the same time inspiring tikkun ("world repair") as his most basic outlook on life. The former without the latter could have led him to be a self-centered actor prone to the drug problems, promiscuity, and so on that abound in show business. The latter without the former could have led him down a path of feeling guilty for his natural talents and sense of playfulness. Instead, from the time he was nine years old, he was acting professionally, tithing a healthy portion of his income to charities, and volunteering for public service announcements whenever he had the opportunity. He moved to Hollywood as soon as he graduated from high school, and although he eventually chose to leave show business, it was there that he met his future wife as well as the martial arts master who would inspire him to earn a black belt and to teach martial arts himself. It was there that he also became a Red Cross relief worker and an emergency medical technician (EMT); this training has enabled him to work part-time on our county rescue squad and bring calmness and compassion to people who are scared or suffering.

Our lives do carve a meaningful path if we allow them to. Each step along the way unfolds itself if we are willing to follow the scent that God may implant in us through our interests and talents. God is not outside our inclinations and passions. Krishna reminds us, "Wherever you see greatness, that is the greatness of God." But rarely do we see greatness in its formative stages. That's why we must trust our talents and inclinations. When Joseph Campbell first used the phrase "Follow your bliss," he discussed it in a very different light than the one suggested by pop culture's expansion of it to "Follow your bliss and the money will follow." Nothing could have been further from Campbell's mind than to imply that following one's bliss would lead to worldly success. To the contrary, he was saying we must follow our passions, our inclinations or callings, even if they lead us into lifelong poverty or social scorn. Campbell was using the phrase as a serious call to duty, not as an invitation to an easy or whimsical path.

Mozart or Ray Charles or Bob Dylan, for example, would obviously have devoted their lives to music whether they made money at it or not. Music was their calling, their muse. Many of the greatest artists throughout history were virtually unknown and impoverished during their own lifetime, or even despised and persecuted. Joseph Campbell's encouragement to follow one's bliss is no different from Krishna's saying, "Do your own *dharma,* even if it seems devoid of merit." Following one's bliss or dharma requires courage, and a willingness to sometimes be thoroughly rejected even by people we love. But life will be on our side. Truth will be on our side. A meaningful life will be on our side.

Sita and I spent many years being considered foolish and irresponsible by most of the members of both our families. Practicing meditation when it was considered silly or even cultish, preaching compassion to killers and bank robbers and rapists, bringing our innocent child into prisons with us, living in ashrams, having no health insurance, working for poverty-level wages or less—we were not exactly the pride of the family tree.

Did we mind? Of course we did. It feels lousy to be looked down upon, but that's no reason to abandon a true calling, whether it is service work, or dance, art, music, or activism. God speaks to us through our callings. We are lucky when we see such a clear path, so it is almost like spitting in God's face to reject it.

The truth is, any vocation or avocation that does not harm others can be of service to the world—a life of tikkun, or world repair. The immense, exquisite tapestry of life is beyond our imagining, and it contains threads of every color and description. Discovering which thread we are called to be, and then being that thread, regardless of consequences—that is what it means to follow our bliss. A Hasidic rabbi of the last century, Zusya of Hanipol, remarked that when he dies and stands before God, God will not ask him, "Why were you not Moses?" But God may indeed ask him, "Why were you not Zusya?"

A Practice: STOPPING

Many people reading this chapter may say, "It sounds great to have a calling like Mozart or Dylan, but I don't really have any passions or natural talents to lead me into my bliss. How do I find my life's path if I have no specific interests to follow?" There are a lot of workshops offered about finding one's creativity and so forth, but I strongly suspect the answer is right in front of our noses: just stop doing so many things, and see what arises in that open, empty space. Most of us hardly stop long enough to eat, let alone to commune intuitively with our inmost leadings.

I cannot tell you what to do, but I can tell you that if you make time for spiritual practice, your own life will lead you onward. Practice strengthens the intuitive system like certain herbs strengthen the immune system. The following are some of our options for stopping in our tracks. You can add your own.

- In the spiritual community in which I live, we *stop* speaking at 9:00 each night.
- During our workday we practice mindfulness, which is simply to *stop* thinking or speaking of anything other than the task at hand.
- When conflicts arise, we come together not to accuse, but expressly to *stop* feeling ill will and distrust so that we can see beyond self-protection and tangential symbols.
- Our morning and evening meditation practice is the most challenging form of stopping. First we seat the body in a way that enables us to *stop* moving or fidgeting. Then we *stop* looking around. Finally we strive as best we can to *stop* perceiving ourselves through the usual ceaseless mental chatter we have grown accustomed to.

In fact, most of the great spiritual commandments, precepts, and teachings throughout history have been merely guidelines for what we should stop. Most of the ten commandments start with "Thou shalt not"; the Buddhist precepts and Hindu Yamas and Niyamas start with "non-," as in non-killing, non-stealing, non-lying. Contemporary people have often complained that the ancient teachings are too negative, but the reason they are phrased negatively is that there really isn't anything to do in order to realize the Divine Presence, the natural Holiness life offers. We have merely to stop thinking and acting in ways that are harmful or selfish or off the mark.

The great teachings unanimously emphasize that all the peace, wisdom, and joy in the universe are already within us; we don't have to gain, develop, or attain them. Like a child standing in a beautiful park with his eyes shut tight, there's no need to imagine trees, flowers, deer, birds, and sky; we merely need to open our eyes and realize what is already here, who we already are—as soon as we stop pretending we're small or unholy.

I could characterize nearly any spiritual practice as simply being: identify and stop, identify and stop, identify and stop. Identify the myriad forms of limitation and delusion we place upon ourselves, and muster the courage to stop each one. Little by little deep inside us, the diamond shines, the eyes open, the dawn rises, we become what we already are. *Tat Twam Asi* (Thou Art That).

Mistaken Identity

What is the relationship of my job to my life? What if my career is really important to me but doesn't seem directly related to "meaningfulness"? Do I have to change jobs? How can I balance my work life and my nonwork life?

Not everyone has a calling or singular passion, yet we still need to earn a livelihood, and we're fools if we do not enjoy ourselves while we do. Making our work more meaningful and enjoyable is a popular subject for books and workshops these days. We can find effective suggestions regarding mindfulness practices, improving workplace relationships, communicating with supervisors and bosses, setting boundaries between work life and private life, getting what we want from our career. Sometimes we can put some of those ideas and techniques into practice and get just what we hoped for, because for all its frustrations or limitations, our job or career is a pretty good fit.

But some of us, as years roll by, begin to feel that we have just been applying Band-Aids to an oozing wound. We suspect we have copped out on ourselves, toiled the best years of our lives away for no deeper reason than the money involved, or our laziness in not wanting to chart a whole different course. Regretting the way we have spent most of the actual hours of our life is a terrible thing to experience. It is one enormous factor of midlife crisis. To avoid this dilemma, it is a good idea to question our job or career every now and then, and be willing to face the truth and act on it no matter what that means. Many of us will discover that we really do like what we do for a living, and that's a very helpful realization to refresh every few years. But some of us will discover that we do not feel satisfied by the work we do, and it then becomes essential to muster enough faith and courage to make some big changes. Our happiness is worth the effort.

I have a friend who is a psychiatrist. He hates psychiatry. He has no respect for the entire profession, and he does not believe that psychiatrists truly help people. He sincerely believes that nearly any other sort of care and attention would help those same people far more than psychiatry does, for a lot less money. But he's hooked on his $40,000 Mercedes. He's hooked on his affluence. He hates his life. He has told me he feels like a whore and an addict. But he is unwilling to give up the familiar—even though it keeps him in misery—in order to leap into the unknown.

It is profoundly sad not to believe in what we do. The two main questions we must ask ourselves in regard to work are these:

1. Is this a good fit for me?
2. Do I believe it benefits the world?

If we cannot answer yes to both, then we are not in the right line of work. One yes will still lead to regrets later on. Imagine the predicament of people like my friend, whose answers are a resounding no to both questions.

In his classic book *The Prophet,* Kahlil Gibran wrote,

"Work is Love made visible." We need to be able to truthfully say that about our job or career. Saying "My career is really important to me" is quite different from this, because we may have all sorts of questionable psychological associations between self-worth and career that are not in our best interests to perpetuate.

The reason I keep saying "job *or* career" is that the two do not have to be one and the same. When our primary interests in life are not the way we earn money, we just need to live simply enough so that any modest job can support us, and we can choose to love that job, and do it well. For the first ten or fifteen years of our prison work, Sita and I needed to augment our income with several part-time jobs. I made wooden toys to sell at craft fairs, plowed gardens all over town, wrote a few articles and book reviews; Sita worked at a deli, made custom stained-glass windows, worked at a stained-glass shop. None of the things we did for money felt like our careers. But they were enjoyable ways to support ourselves and added a little beauty to the world, so we would definitely have answered yes to the questions above. They also afforded us the time to pursue our main work.

Our era has a very unusual slant on this concept called career. Career has become the accepted hub around which virtually everything else revolves. We often choose career over our own health. We may choose career over our mates and children. We choose career over our time to study, pray, walk, hike, meditate, participate in community life. We fuss over our children's potential careers like it's the most important aspect of life. If our children want to take a year or two off between high school and college, we freak out. We worry they'll get behind. What does that mean? Behind what?

Career is not deep enough to be the center of everyone's life. Career is not who we are. It is something we do for thirty or forty years and then we stop. If we think it's the hub of life, then we devalue childhood and old age—which, of course, we have obviously done: focusing our children's lives around educational training toward a desirable career, and shuffling our retired people off to nursing homes or retirement villages.

One British study showed that men who retired were almost twice as likely to die within five years as those who continued working! Isn't that a sad, foolish, and unnecessary case of mistaken identity? Career is not the be-all and end-all of a human life. There are happy, kind people in virtually every field, and there are miserable, self-centered people in virtually every field. Career guarantees nothing, and it hardly scratches the surface of who we are.

This fixation of ours is a very recent phenomenon. As recently as sixty or seventy years ago, if you were to say to my grandfather, "So, Ben, tell me, what do you do?" he would probably have looked at you quizzically and said, "I do many things." There's no chance he would have understood what you were getting at. If you persisted and said, "No, I mean, how do you make a living?" he would have probably replied, "What do you care?" It wasn't considered very important. What was important was his place in the community, in the synagogue; what was important were the integrity and honor of his family and their reputation.

What my grandfather, a pillar of his community, actually did for a living was to paint houses. My grand-uncle collected rags and sold them to rag dealers. Both were highly successful human beings. To them, what they did for money was the pettiest part of life. No blue-collar/white-collar divisions. So long as it was honest, who cared? And they worked as little as possible. If you had approached them with a plan for doubling the size of their businesses and hiring employees to do the work, they would have thought you were crazy. Why would they want all that bother? They needed to feed their families, pay the rent, help the poor in their neighborhood, have a little fun; what else did they need from a livelihood? So they painted houses and collected rags, loved their work and did it well.

As hard as it is to comprehend in the context of today's consumption-oriented society, many people in times gone by were not interested in becoming wealthy or even financially secure. Character and virtue and wisdom and joy were the mark of a person, not one's choice of career. Contentment used to be a virtue. A lack of materialistic ambition was not such a bad thing. Remember these sayings: "Man does not live by bread alone" and "The best things in life are free." Our humanity is always the most important common career we all share—our career of kindness. Anything else we do is just part of the support system for that connection of kindness between us.

There need not be any conflict between our worldly and spiritual success. The key is to be honest enough with ourselves to pursue a balance that suits our own unique natures. We don't have to be Bill Gates, and neither do we have to imitate Mother Teresa. We need to accept personal responsibility for finding productive work in our lives— work that reflects our ambitions, our compassion, and even our playfulness.

No career will create such well-rounded success automatically. It's up to each of us to do that for ourselves, and it is not necessarily a one-shot deal. Life may have more twists and turns for us than we would ever expect, but that's what makes it an adventure. The main price of admission is to keep our tastes and demands modest enough that we can follow the trail wherever it leads us rather than staying behind clutching our air conditioners. We may keep the same career our whole lives or look back on a wide variety of jobs, but our choices can be conscious and deliberate, and we can fully enjoy the whole adventure.

A Practice: WORK/LIFE VISION QUEST

Set aside an evening or a Sunday for sincere reflection about your job or career. Have pen and paper handy so you can make some notes or lists. Begin your practice with a half-hour meditation and then a brief prayer/invocation along these lines:

> May God bless me with guidance and insight about my work life. I offer my willingness to see the truth even if I don't like what I see. I ask for courage to follow the truth that is revealed to me.

However you word it yourself, a proper invocation is your way of joining forces with your spiritual guides and professing your willingness to face the truth. Native American traditions used these principles of invocation in many ceremonies, including the vision quest. Anytime you step back from the busy flow of your life in order to gain insight about where you are headed, you are embarking on a vision quest. Respect it as such, and ask for help.

As in the practice of clarifying your values on page 139, first clarify the two major questions about your current job given earlier in this chapter and don't rush yourself:

1. Is this a good fit for me?
2. Do I believe it benefits the world?

- **Continue here if both answers are yes:**
  If your answers are yes, then begin listing the best and worst parts of your job, and leave space below each item so you can brainstorm how to better appreciate and perform the best parts, and how to change or embrace the worst parts. You have already acknowledged that you are in a suitable job, so it makes sense to examine the parts that make you grumble, and figure out a way either not to do them at all or to surrender your resistance and do them with love. Staying in-between is what causes ulcers, heart problems, and stress.

  Make an inventory of your time as well. List the things that are important to you in your job, your family life, your hobbies or other pursuits, and take an honest look at whether you are giving at least a little time to all of them. If you are not, then again, either brainstorm a way to schedule them in or admit to yourself that you are choosing to abandon that pastime. For example, I once made a list of all the things that were important for me to do every day: a morning hike, working out with weights, playing guitar and piano, reading, meditation, yoga, office work, and several other things as well. It became instantly clear that I would need about a thirty-hour day to get in all my requirements. For years, I had been playing a foolish game with myself, always feeling like I was not managing my time well enough, when the truth was that my expectations were completely unrealistic.

  Seeing this in black and white, I was able to admit that maybe I could only play piano a couple times a week, and maybe I had to alternate my hikes with my workouts, and so forth. Maybe there were some things I was trying to hold on to that I had even lost enthusiasm for, and needed to discard. The whole process helped me feel more deliberate about my choices, instead of always feeling an underlying level of frustration that I was neglecting something or other. One more prime source of stress removed.

The final part of your work vision quest can be a rededication of your energies, your gratitude, your determination to do your work impeccably and joyfully. Bring to mind your usual demeanor at work, and critique yourself. Do you gossip more than you like? Do you manipulate others, or brownnose people in authority? Do you express resentment or show bias toward a particular person? Be willing to see and wince. Let yourself feel how much you do not like certain things about your work personality, and resolve to change them.

Scan also the things you like most about your work persona. Are you skilled? Considerate? Generous with your time? Willing to share credit? Happy to lend a hand? Be willing to feel good about what you do well, and resolve to continue, whether or not you feel you are appreciated fully. Understand that you do these things because they reflect who you are, not because other people will approve or reciprocate.

Occasionally taking the time to sort through our feelings and actions like this can reduce stress by the bucketful. A lot of what we call stress is simply unresolved tensions, or "fence-sitting"—elements of our lives we do not take the time to be deliberate about. After a vision quest like this, you may return to work with renewed energy and even a greater sense of playfulness.

- **Continue here if either answer is no:**

  If the blunt truth is that you either do not fit well in the work you are doing, or you feel your work is not what Buddhists would call "right livelihood" (being uplifting to the world even in a very modest way), then you have a life problem, not a work problem. It is poison to stay in a job you do not believe in, no matter how high your salary or how compelling your circumstances. Use the rest of this vision quest to uncover the conflicts within you that lead you to disrespect your time so badly.

  You may want to list, on the one hand, the reasons you feel reluctant or frightened to leave your job; and, on the other hand, the range of opportunities you could explore as an alternative. Take a very thoughtful look at both those lists, and think about how to ensure meaningfulness in your life.

  You may be daunted by some of the risks you may have to take or the luxuries you may need to sacrifice if you change your direction, but please consider what you are already sacrificing by spending your workweek doing something that doesn't feel right for you. Do you have faith that there is something more right for you to do? If not, why not? Remember, life is not chaotic; it is ordered and intelligent. Even the tiniest flea has a digestive system and a heart. Does it sound reasonable that you, who are so much more intricately designed, were meant to merely waste your time and then die?

  The final part of your vision quest may be to muster your courage for a change of life, and take at least the beginning steps in a practical plan to do so. The first step may be a conversation with your family about selling the boat, giving up the time-share at the shore, and whatever else came up on your list of reasons you have been keeping a job you don't believe in. Try, by the closing prayer of your vision quest, to commit yourself to making reasonable forward motion toward a better job or career. Despite any sacrifices, you will not regret doing what you feel is right, or at least ceasing to do what you feel is not right. This is of crucial importance to your spiritual journey.

One for All, All for One

———— 🌿 ————

How do I balance individual fulfillment with my responsibilities and obligations to society? Isn't the point of living in a democracy like ours that we can all pursue whatever individual goals we want? That we can cultivate our individuality?

In November of 1969, Sita and I crewed on an ocean-going trimaran sailboat that got caught in Hurricane Martha in the Caribbean. We battled the storm for three days and nights, but finally, exhausted and battered, we hid behind a little island off the northwest coast of Cuba. The next day we were spotted by a military patrol and captured by the Cuban army. During several hours of interrogation, one of the most interesting exchanges I had with the Cuban officers, and which I have reflected on from time to time since, went something like this:

"Where were you sailing?"

"We're headed toward Jamaica."

"For what purpose?"

"No purpose. The captain built this boat, and my wife and I are his crew."

"But why are you doing this?"

"Because we want to."

"What good are you accomplishing for your society?"

"No good at all."

"Then why would your government allow you to do this?"

"Because we are free to do as we want."

"What about your families?"

"Our families have nothing to do with it."

"But why would you want to do this?"

"Well, you might say we're trying to find ourselves."

"Find yourselves? What does that mean?"

At the time, I was deeply moved by the Cubans' sincerity and innocence, and simultaneously delighted that I was an American and could do as I pleased. They could not fathom an individual's soul-journey beyond the social order. I could not fathom such absolute obligation to the common good. At the time, I assumed I saw the situation clearly and they didn't. In the thirty-some years since that interrogation, I have come to feel that my position was no more valid than theirs. We were both blind to the beautiful part of each other's situation. They were a product of their indoctrination to live solely for the state, and I was no less a product of my indoctrination to live solely for individual fulfillment. What the Buddha called "The Middle Way" would be somewhere in between.

Any good idea can be gradually misconstrued and distorted to the point that it not only ceases to be a good idea but actually becomes an extremely bad one. This is how many cults are formed. That's what often happens in revolutions like Cuba's, and that's what I feel has happened with regard to our Western notion of freedom, and especially the cruel mirage of personal freedom. Freedom does not mean that I can decide I want my stomach to pump blood and my heart to digest food. Physical laws exist that are not negotiable. By the same token, spiritual laws exist as well, and therefore freedom also does not mean that I can be ignorant or selfish or vain or cruel without suffering adverse consequences.

Besides the laws that do not change, there also exist needs, which change constantly. My father's last four months of life were not subject to my convenience. It was not optional to either embrace or ignore the Great Depression that began in 1929. My body at age fifty-three requires different considerations than my body at age thirty.

True freedom exists firmly within the bounds of natural laws and the shifting needs of our lives. Many of the unhappiest and most deranged people throughout history have been kings, queens, emperors, dictators, rock stars, movie stars, business tycoons, and others who became so wealthy or popular or powerful that they fancied they were above the laws of nature as well as the laws of man. They were free to do as they chose at any hour of the day or night. Every shred of relevant historical evidence shows that a human being does not do well with such an unnatural degree of personal choice. Freedom is a good thing. Unchecked personal choice is not; it usually drives people crazy. Yet that is exactly what we have enshrined in place of true freedom. We have been taught to revere and pursue it unquestioningly.

Human beings exist in relation to each other. Real freedom cannot be separated from responsiveness to others. To be free means to be able to respond to the needs of the moment within the basic rules of a good life. Let's say that I walk by a lake where a child is drowning; I may passionately want to save her, but I don't have the freedom to do it if I don't know how to swim. I may have a million dollars in my pocket, I may be president of the United States, but if I haven't learned how to swim, that child will still drown.

Even the sincerest motivation is only one part of freedom. Freedom requires skills and capability; it requires availability and goodwill and common sense.

If we are unskilled, self-centered, addicted, or greedy, we will not be very free. Merely doing what we want, in a way that ignores our connection with each other or the best interests of society, isn't personal freedom. It's time to start looking at this bill of goods we've been sold about personal freedom. We need to see that many of the attitudes that we may consider to be universal truths are in reality just flawed tenets of our cult of individualism.

INDIVIDUALISM VERSUS INDIVIDUALITY

Many of us have spent time in third world countries, where people don't have the freedom of choice that we have in this country. At an early age they begin being responsible for helping their families and communities function. They have obligations and duties that most of us would call severe limitations on their personal freedom. It is ironic that people in those cultures often seem to have a higher personal happiness quotient, and happier families and communities, than many Americans have. They don't always feel oppressed. We may think, "Boy, they're really prisoners. They have to go into whatever trade their father or mother is in. I wouldn't want to be limited like that. I like having all the options in the world."

But options to do what? To fool ourselves into thinking we can be everything or do everything? To stay so busy that we never feel a moment of peace or contentment? To disconnect ourselves so harshly from the needs of our families and communities that we cut off the very source of our sense of belonging? We need to be honest and say, "How are we doing as a society with our models of success and personal freedom? Are we happy yet?"

Individuality is real and effortless. Like snowflakes, we are unique individuals. We don't have to dye our hair green or pierce our eyelids to assert our individuality. We are born with it, just as we are. Individualism, like any other "ism," is conceptual; it's man-made. It is neither real nor effortless. It requires constant propping up.

We need to reevaluate the principles by which we're living. "Contentment" is regarded mostly negatively now, as though it meant "lack of drive." Many other words that have traditionally carried positive connotations are now spoken with dread or derision: Duty. Sacrifice. Deference. Reverence. Obedience. Modesty. These words abound in every wisdom tradition and religion, yet we act as though they are outdated.

We must begin to be less arrogant, and turn back to the ancient truths. Giving your life to your community or family can be a joyous expression of trust in the process of life itself. We now identify our personal agendas as being our lives—what we want to be; what we want to achieve; what we want to do. We don't have faith that our own individual life is an exquisite tapestry of which our free will is only one set of threads, not the whole design. Life will still have direction and meaning if we ease up on pursuing our personal freedom. It can be a wonderful feeling to let go of something that we really thought we wanted and say, "Lord, may I be an instrument of your peace."

We may think, "I thought I was going to be pursuing that degree, but working with those kids really seems to be important, so I'll keep doing that for a while instead. They need me."

As time goes by and we follow our lives rather than always lead them, we begin to feel levels of relief that are un-believable. We say, "Ah, the joy not to be so personally in-volved in my life anymore, but to be involved with these ageless principles of living simply, doing spiritual practice, and trying to be of service. What a relief not to have to cre-ate my own life all by myself!" We may very well go back to school or carve out a career. We may still end up with that degree, but only because we believe that it's the best way we can contribute. We do it because the world needs doctors and plumbers, teachers and truck drivers. And we love the world, and begin to intuit our place in it.

Then the puzzle starts fitting better—with all the people around us, and the problems in our community, and in the world. Maybe we wind up doing a different part of it than we thought we'd do, but it's a team effort, and we have obligations and responsibilities—to our family, our com-munity, our country, our world, to the spiritual journey.

Obligations and responsibilities are an important com-ponent of a good life; they are not merely burdens. Human beings tend to fall apart when they run out of duties and obligations. Even though they may sometimes be demand-ing, our duties help us to feel a part of the people around us rather than apart from them.

A Practice: THE BREATH OF LIFE

The Lord God formed man from the dust of the ground and breathed into his nostrils the breath of life, and the man became a living being.

—Genesis 2:7

One of the most direct routes to acknowledging your common humanity in the moment is to become aware of your own breath. From the Hebrew *ruach* to the Hindu *prana,* breath is intimately linked with spirit in all the great traditions. From a scientific standpoint, breath distinguishes a corpse from a living person. From a spiritual standpoint, breath conveys the living spirit of God. From a social standpoint, we all breathe the same air. From the beginning of recorded spiritual history, seekers have worked with the breath in order to quiet the mind, calm or even heal the body, or change consciousness to commune with the Divine. Many of these techniques are still known today. Most use some degree of visualization. Some are extremely technical and considered dangerous if performed casually or without proper motivation. But most are simple and safe, like the one I have included here.

The Buddha originally taught the following technique, which has been updated over the centuries, most recently by the late American Sufi master Murshid Samuel L. Lewis (known popularly as "Sufi Sam"). I've revised it only slightly from his adaptation:

- Begin by becoming aware of the in-breath and out-breath. Then breathe in a heavy breath and be aware that you're breathing in a heavy breath; breathe out a heavy breath and be aware that you're breathing out a heavy breath. Do this a few times.
- Then breathe in a gentle breath, aware you're breathing in a gentle breath, and breathe out a gentle breath, aware you're breathing out a gentle breath. Breathe in a short breath, out a short breath. Breathe in a long breath, out a long breath.
- After doing each of these a few times, gradually make your breath long and gentle, long and refined. For the

rest of this practice, attentively breathe in and out this long, refined breath. On this breath, breathe in all the joy you're capable of breathing in and breathe out all the joy you're capable of breathing out. Joy in and joy out. Do this for a few minutes.

• Then breathe in all the love you're capable of breathing in and all the love you're capable of breathing out. Love in and love out. Finally make the breath even gentler, even longer and more penetrating, and breathe in all the peace you're capable of breathing in and all the peace you're capable of breathing out. Peace in and peace out. As you do this, fill the room with peace. Fill your home or neighborhood with peace. Breathe peace for the whole city, for the whole world in which you live.

... The Other Tastes Salt

I deeply want to have a healthy and happy marriage, but I get very confused when we have such a hard time getting along. How can I tackle the larger issues of service and community life when I can barely handle the one-on-one community of married life?

Let there be such oneness between us that when one cries, the other tastes salt.

—Rosabelle Belleve

The goal of our life should not be to find joy in marriage, but to bring more love and truth into the world. We marry to assist each other in this task.

—Leo Tolstoy

The passages above address the two important prongs of any discussion about marriage. First, Belleve points to the awesome depth of intimacy that is possible between two people—"when one cries, the other tastes salt." Imagine that. On balance, Tolstoy reminds us that marital self-centeredness is no loftier than individual self-centeredness. As individuals or as a couple, he exhorts us to remember that our purpose is "to bring more love and truth into the world," not just to have an enjoyable life with one other person.

It may sound as though those two views are in conflict. But Tolstoy would have no problem with Belleve's statement, so long as both husband and wife don't stop there. We can use such profound oneness as a springboard into the big Profound Oneness. In other words, we would be heading for the day when we could say, "When anyone cries, we both taste salt." That's the love of the sages and saints. That's the potential of marriage as a path of service in the large community of the world.

Few, if any, phenomena in life are as precious as thirty, forty, or even fifty or more years of a genuinely good marriage. It is a profound blessing to the two people involved, and a service to the world as well. This is worth a tremendous amount of work. It is a shame that so many people, due merely to shortsightedness, fail to ever experience such intimacy. But it is not out of reach; most people have just lost touch with what a lifelong marriage requires. Forget about boundaries and separate identities. Marriage is alchemy, not psychology. It is a spiritual path, not a business contract. Marriage is a means for total transformation.

A friend once asked, "You and Sita and Josh have such a close family life. What's the secret?"

My response was, "All three of us love the spiritual path more than we love each other." Even as it came out of my mouth, I could hear how awful that sounded in our contemporary culture. Wasn't I supposed to say, "We love each other more than anything else?" But the truth is, personal love is forever lacking unless Divine Love is the priority.

Loving God, truth, dharma, the path, the most, is what gives a proper context to the love we have for each other. Without a proper context, personal love can become possessive love, which is one of the major highways to hell. *Baby, I love you more than anything. I would do anything for you. I don't care about anyone else in the world. You're all I ever think about.* Watch out. Better be prepared to run for cover when you start disappointing that person.

Possessive love never ends well unless it matures with time and effort. It is emotion without intelligence. Emotion is wonderful when guided and controlled by wisdom, but without it, it's as dangerous as a sports car careening all over the highway with the driver fast asleep. A serious wreck is just a matter of time.

> I like your smile and your fingertips, I like the way that you move your lips. I like the cool way you look at me. Everything about you is bringing me misery.
>
> —Bob Dylan, "Buckets of Rain"

THE HEART OF GOD

Practicing love as a path of service is a very powerful process. You allow your love for your mate or children to bring out the best in you, and then you keep your best out front for everyone and everything. Be more generous to the panhandler because you're in love. Be quicker to forgive the person who is annoying or rude or angry, because you're in love. Be more in awe of nature, more appreciative of art, music, and poetry, because you're in love. Allow love to awaken you to all of life rather than fixate you toward one person.

Self-centered love is contractive and possessive, while spiritual love is expansive and generous. Romance and marriage can lead either way, so it is extremely important for us to consider these things as we "fall in love," and hopefully before we get married. If one of a couple wants the small love and one the Big Love, there are bound to be some big problems up ahead. That doesn't mean the problems can't be surmounted after getting married, but with a 50 percent divorce rate in our culture, it is a good idea to face such differences beforehand if we have enough awareness to ask the questions.

love or LOVE

Of course, the popular sentiment in our day and age is toward small love, not Big Love. To practice love and marriage as a spiritual path requires a lot of insight—the couple must see through many layers of popular myth and sentimentality—and the courage to buck the trends again and again and again.

However much we adore our mate's body, looks, youthfulness, or vigor, all of those things change in time. There's nothing wrong with a husband and wife trying to keep their sexual passion alive. Judaism advises us that enjoying each other sexually is one of the duties of a marriage and a gift from God. It may help to keep us happy and balanced, so that we are better members of our community. Where we fall off the path is seeing our physical relationship as the whole thing or even the most important part.

Look at the actor Christopher Reeve, who played Superman in several movies in the 1980s. One moment he's big, muscular, healthy, and gorgeous, and the next moment he suffers a fall while riding his horse and breaks his neck, never to walk again. His beautiful wife goes from being his passionate romantic partner to being his primary caregiver. Their marriage becomes a path of service for her to a degree she never could have imagined. And because of her love and support, he too is able to forge a path of service promoting spinal-injury research. This couple has allowed their compassion and commitment to each other to spill over into compassion and commitment to many others. That's the way marriage can work.

This is not to say it was a wonderful thing that happened, or that Reeve and his wife are happy as larks. No couple hopes for something like that. They must have been terrified when it first happened. Maybe they're still terrified. But the marriage vows cover it, don't they? *In sickness and in health, so long as you both shall live.* The vows are not vague or ambiguous. Married life is not predictable or safe. Your spouse is the person with whom you may experience the greatest—and sometimes most tragic or hair-raising—challenges of your life. Please try to embrace this open-ended view *before* getting married.

How does this path actually work? How does marriage open us up and prepare us to bear the force of God's own love? Two main processes come to mind, one involving love from our spouse and the other involving love toward our children.

FEELING WHAT IT'S LIKE
TO BE LOVED BY GOD

As we fall in love romantically, the other person looks at us and sees the very best. Their friends may look at us and say,

"What's the big deal?" But our beloved looks at us and says, "Can't you see? She (or he) is so beautiful, so genuine, so deep, so wonderful!"

What we see in each other is true, but of course it is not the full story. If we move in with each other, if we get married, if we stay together enough years, we will also see the lowest and worst parts of each other; the selfish side, the fearful side, the petty and weak, the dysfunctional and even perverted sides. If we really open up to each other, we cannot see only what is pretty.

If our mate continues to love us even after we have long since tumbled off the pedestal she or he put us on when we met, even after we have shamed and humiliated ourselves and done things we can never take back, then something begins to dawn in us: God sees everything too. If a human being can still love us through all our crap, then maybe God loves us as well. Accepting this love for the totality of who we are could be the most profound realization of our life.

FEELING WHAT IT'S LIKE TO LOVE AS GOD LOVES

So we can use the experience of our partner's love to help us feel what it is like to be loved by God. But it is almost impossible to feel God's own part of it until we have a child. We may have developed unconditional love and forgiveness for our mate, but it probably took a lot of work. Our mate has let us down, even betrayed us. Our mate has the power to hurt us. There's always going to be some effort required in loving our spouse through the rough times.

But our love for a baby is as effortless as God's love for us. We look down into that crib and see an angel who needs us and trusts us and depends on us for everything. We see the clear eyes of a soul who sees no wrong in us to forgive, no weakness to overlook, no power over us except the power of pure love. The contact is soul to soul, with no personal history or other obstacles in the way. Without a second's hesitation, we would step in front of a train for that baby.

Our love for an infant may be as close as a human being can be to loving as God loves. As that baby grows up and develops a selfish or petty side, we don't see a selfish or petty person; we see instead our beautiful baby who means well but is caught up in some problems. Even if our baby someday lands on death row, we say, "He really isn't a bad person. Underneath all his problems, he's really good." And we are absolutely right. That's how God sees us.

> The lowest of the low you can think of, is dearer
> to me than your only son is to you.
> —Ba'al Shem Tov

I wish every good thing for my child. I hurt when he hurts, I rejoice when he is happy. It is never too late for him to ask my forgiveness if he really means it. I look at him and see into his heart. I know that no matter what, he has goodness in him. This is the natural disposition of a parent toward a child; it is not forced or philosophical. This is how God loves. This is where marriage and family life can take us if we understand them as a spiritual path.

THE SERVICE OF LETTING GO

If marriage helps us to love as God loves, we must also bear in mind that "God so loved the world, he gave his only begotten son." That is to say, marriage also gives us the profound mystery of bearing the excruciating grief of losing each other; we can bear this pain in a way that does not act surprised or outraged or bitter over the natural rhythms of life and death. This is a valuable aspect of service in a culture that worships youth and tends to run from pain or loss.

> Love, to be real, it must cost—it must hurt—it must empty us of self.
>
> —Mother Teresa

For example, look at me and Sita. People have said they envy our marriage and that now, after so many years, it must be so easy for us. The ego dramas do fade away, but when Sita looks into my face now she sees a gray-haired, grandfatherly man instead of the young stud she married. My hearing isn't what it used to be. My vision isn't what it used to be. My stamina isn't what it used to be. Our son is often concerned about my health.

It is beginning to dawn on us that this is no joke; after weathering countless storms with each other, one of us is going to lose the other to time. When one of us dies, it will seem much too soon no matter when it happens. If you think eighty is a fitting age to lose a mate, just ask a couple of happy seventy-nine-year-olds whether they agree.

I was nineteen when we got married. We have been married virtually our whole lives. We have always worked together, spent nearly twenty-four hours a day with each other, raised a child together, seen the world together, shared one taste in music, humor, movies, books, and scriptures, nursed each other through serious illnesses. We can't conceive of a world without each other in it. The names Bo and Sita are spoken together so routinely that people some-times write it as one person: Boensita Lozoff. Can you imagine the grief of the survivor?

If this softens your heart a little, then our marriage con-tinues to be a path of service even now, as we consider the grief it will bring when one of us is widowed. The funda-mental reality of a life of service is always an openhearted connection to others, not just in joy but in sorrow as well. Our joys and sorrows unite us with the joys and sorrows of all people. To close off and label them "private" is to miss their purpose. Our life itself is our friendship with the world.

This is what it means for marriage to be a path of service. Two people become one couple. They serve the world in how they manage their marriage as much as any activism they may engage in. They wear rings on one particular fin-ger so that anyone can recognize at a glance that they're not just individuals anymore. It's no less of a symbol than monks wearing robes to identify themselves as people who have chosen a full-time, committed spiritual path.

This is the potential marriage holds. Don't settle for less. You can know what it means to truly taste the salt of your beloved's tears. And then you can begin to understand what it means to taste the salt of the world's tears. From that place comes true compassion, and a deep desire to be of ser-vice to the world. These are qualities that saints from every tradition have told us are the keys to the Kingdom of Heaven.

A Practice: DAILY MARRIAGE VOWS

Sita and I do this practice at the beginning of each day. We face each other and clasp hands, look directly into each other's eyes, and say,

> May I truly cherish you today, knowing this may be our last day together.

After a few seconds, we usually touch foreheads gently for a moment, release hands and bow to each other, and then go on about our day. It's a very useful and powerful practice.

Believe it or not, although it may sound like it would get stale, daily repetition is actually a way to keep vows fresh. Those few seconds give us an opportunity to be very serious about the truth both of our relationship and of life itself. Is this our last day together? No one ever knows, but for about two hundred thousand people each day, it turns out to be. Better safe than sorry. And of course, these vows can be exchanged between any two people who wish to remind themselves to cherish each other, married or not.

The Fortress of Anger

Being patient and even kind to strangers often is easier than showing simple tolerance for those I live with. How can I work on my most important relationships and not keep losing my temper with those I love?

"Familiarity breeds contempt." The old saying is not a curse, but can certainly serve as a warning to watch out for this phenomenon, which human beings can so easily fall prey to. The people we most wish to cherish can be the ones we treat the most miserably.

Over many years of doing spiritual practice, I noticed that I would lose my temper less often, and at fewer people. That makes sense, right? However, the confusing part was that when I did lose my temper, the anger was just as intense or even more intense than ever! Also, the people I was most likely to blow up at were the people I loved the most—Sita, Josh. I even screamed at my mother once, just a half hour before giving a church service on inner peace! I felt so ashamed.

Isn't that strange? If meditation, prayer, and clean living were whittling away at the rage inside of me, why wouldn't the intensity of anger decline along with the frequency? And why wouldn't my sweet little family be the first ones off the hook, instead of the last ones to benefit from the fruits of my spiritual practice?

Perhaps it is not so strange after all. A great deal of anger had surely dissolved through my spiritual development; it was no sham. But who more than our family members can trigger our deepest doubts and insecurities, and unearth the "uncooked seeds" of any old hang-ups that still remain? As for the intensity of anger, everything becomes more powerful along the course of our spiritual awakening, which is a very good reason to make sure we are steadfastly trying to dismantle the underpinnings of anger at its source.

Anger can have a very powerful grip on us. However, if we can see how it works and where it seems to draw its formidable power from, we can begin to free ourselves from its hold. Much modern psychological advice about anger recognizes only two options: repression and expression. Since repression can be unhealthy, many people conclude the expression of anger is essential or even healthy. But spiritual teachings hold repression and expression as being somewhat alike. In both cases, we identify with anger as being ours. According to the wisdom teachings, that is a dangerous, self-defeating illusion. There is a third way, which is to step back and observe more clearly the immediate experience of anger, until we can recognize how it operates, how it seizes control of our free will, and then actually disable it. Pulling one wire from a distributor cap will disable an entire engine. The challenge is to find the distributor cap for anger. This process is different from psychological analysis, which attempts to understand all the parts of the engine.

Committed spiritual practice sometimes affords us an opportunity to see the distributor cap of some of our deepest chronic behavior problems. That's what happened to me concerning anger in the middle of a two-month retreat of silence and partial fasting. I fell into a period of horrifying anger that shook me to my roots, especially since I couldn't scream, shout, or punch the wall. I had to sit with it in silence. Imagine being angrier than you have ever been in your life and having nowhere to go with it except inside yourself. Sitting all day with no distractions, you can't possibly repress or push away anything; you can't turn on the TV or stuff your face or call a friend or go for a walk. It's just you and anger, right there in the moment of truth. Actually, I did lose control and break silence briefly, and then the anger toward myself tripled because I had broken my vow of silence. I fell sobbing on the floor, hating myself, hating my life, hating my confusion at what to do next—so much anger and self-hatred. So much self!

Feeling adrenaline throughout my body, shame and despair in my heart, confusion in my mind, I prayed, "Please, let me see the truth, let me see where this rage comes from, even if I hate what I see. May I see the truth of anger."

At some point an image appeared—I was a small child, being comforted by my mother, apparently after she had lost her temper with me. I was shaking and crying, and she was saying, "Come on now, you know I love you! That's why I get so angry, because I love you so much." And then, as if on a movie marquee, I saw that I was learning "ANGER PROVES LOVE."

Another image appeared. This time it was my whole family—six foul-tempered people—sitting around making excuses about being "passionate" people and actually scoffing at families who were calm and didn't scream at each other. Again, like a neon sign, I saw,

ANGER = PASSION
PASSIONATE = ATTRACTIVE, EXCITING
UNPASSIONATE = DULL, BORING

I began to grasp how many layers of innocently false notions, excuses, and habits underlie our emotional problems. We live according to how we see the world; we see the world to a large degree according to how we were taught. There is no one to blame, but there is a great deal to be corrected.

Looking honestly at my own heart, at my wounds from a lifetime of justifying anger, I said, "I no longer believe in this philosophy that my father was taught as a child, that my mother was taught as a child, that I was taught as a child. I no longer believe that anger proves love. I no longer believer anger is passion. I no longer believe anger makes me a more interesting person. I believe ranting and raving are forms of violence. I believe anger never helps. Please, dear God, allow me to give up anger, as my contribution toward a more peaceful world."

I sat silently awhile, and received various insights and teachings about anger—for example, that anger is not a genuine emotion; it's a distraction. Anger is a smoke screen that takes us away from facing an uncomfortable truth. Many of us use anger to cover up embarrassment. Being angry is easier than admitting that our ego feels threatened or humiliated. Anger directs the attention to another person, or to a convenient enemy like the government, or polluters, or cops, or criminals—anywhere but ourselves.

Much like sexual orgasm, heavy anger is so totally absorbing, it's almost impossible to see through the illusion while we are in it. We don't want to see through it in that moment; we just want to conquer the object of our anger. I know many people who have given up precious years of their lives because of anger. I know decent people sitting on death row because of a moment of uncontrolled anger. That's how tragically captivating it can be.

BUT I'M RIGHT!

If we use anger at injustice as the source of our energy, we may do something harmful, something that we will later regret. . . . Compassion is the only source of energy that is useful and safe. With compassion, your energy is born from insight; it is not blind energy.

—Thich Nhat Hanh

Probably the most difficult type of anger to let go of is what might be called self-righteous anger—when someone else is absolutely, totally wrong and we are absolutely, totally right! Or when someone we care about is hurting themselves and we've got to make him or her see the truth. You know what I'm talking about, don't you? Rising up like Krishna urges Arjuna to do in the Bhagavad Gita, or like Jesus with the moneychangers in the sacred temple. We imagine, "This isn't 'my' anger! This is the Wrath of God at such an obvious injustice!" The problem is, Arjuna's and Jesus' motivation was indeed righteous. But that is a world apart from *self*-righteous anger.

A saint's anger has no ego in it, no personal fears or desires, no neurotic buttons being pushed. It's not self-protective like our anger, but more like a hurricane or tornado—its awesome power isn't "against" us; it's just a mighty force of nature that humbles us and reminds us of our place in God's creation.

Righteous anger humbles, but self-righteous anger puffs up the ego. Righteous anger seeks to defeat the sin, but self-righteous anger scorns the sinner as well. There's a world of difference, I deeply believe that most of us have a long way to go before we can entertain the idea of expressing anger as a positive force in the world. As long as there's a "self," as long as there's someone wondering, "Is anger okay?" then it's a good idea to consider it a dangerous form of expression.

DO YOU REALLY WANT TO LET IT GO?

In the years since my revelations about anger, I've had a chance to feel how big an effect it had on me. I'd love to say I've never gotten angry again and never will, but that's not usually how these things work. Besides whatever else it is, anger is partly a habit, and habits usually take time—and practice—to change. The wires on the distributor cap find ways of reconnecting themselves, but they are the same wires on the same cap, so it becomes fairly routine to reach in and yank them loose again.

This principle also holds true for people who experience being born again or the raising of the *kundalini*, or oneness with God—the ego-minded rushes to proclaim sweeping changes like "I'll never be selfish again," or "I'll never get angry again," or "I'll never desire another cigarette." Then, when the wires reconnect themselves a few weeks later and the people realize those old engines are running again, they get terribly depressed because they conclude their wonderful experience must have been false. The experience may indeed have been genuine, but when the experience is over, that's when personal spiritual practice is needed to stabilize and solidify the transformation.

The times I've gotten angry during this period, I've sat down and tried to see where I was still holding any belief that anger is either real or justified. With one hand I prayed to let go of anger, yet with the other I held on to a teensy bit of it for emergencies, for a false sense of security. I found a tiny part of me saying, "Listen, you'd better hold on to a little bit of anger in such a vicious world! Gotta protect yourself, you know!" So I would sit and look honestly at that, and remind myself, "I no longer believe I need anger; I no longer believe anger protects me." Yank. The wires come off again.

It's amazing how reluctant or even terrified we are of accepting a better, more peaceful life—while seeming to spend all our time seeking it. We are truly our own best friends and worst enemies all at the same time. The very best reason to move beyond anger is simply because it's beneath our dignity. Anger, hatred, revenge, greed, arrogance, addictions, fears, lusts—all are unworthy of us. We are Divine. We are Loved and we are Love. Every one of us embodies the Sacred One. If we act accordingly, we find the profound peace and freedom that make all our effort worthwhile.

A Practice: WORKING WITH ANGER

It is very difficult to exercise self-discipline in the middle of anger, but you can do it. You must move your attention from the object of your anger to the actual process of it instead. Forget who did what to whom. You can deal with that later, when you're calmer and less likely to make things worse. For now, focus on the experience of anger itself as an observer rather than as the hero or the victim.

- As you feel yourself getting angry, stay still, try to breathe more smoothly and a little more deeply (not too deeply, just a little; you don't want to hyperventilate). If you can catch anger in its seed stage, you may be able to work with it in the midst of whatever conflict you are engaged in without it getting the best of you. But if necessary, excuse yourself from the presence of your "anger partner" in order to do this work. You can resolve the conflict later.

- Allow yourself to feel the tightness in your stomach, neck, and shoulders, the bitterness, the adrenaline, the indignant "rightness," the unfairness and injustice huffing and puffing around in your head.

- Next, become aware of the terrible separateness that anger creates, not just between you and the object of your anger, but between you and your own body, between you and the whole universe. In other words, study what anger really feels like in all its aspects.

- Now, as you allow all these awful feelings to come into awareness, remind yourself, "Anger feels terrible! All people feel this at one time or another. May this help me to be more understanding and compassionate. May I use this experience to identify with *everyone's* anger. May it humble me and help me feel what I have in common with all beings."

- Finally, if you know someone who is especially angry much of the time, take a moment to focus on him or her specifically with a prayer of goodwill, such as, "May this experience help me to be more compassionate to so-and-so. May it remove some of his anger." Hold the image of that person as clearly as you can, and try to remove his anger by seeing his tightness relax and his face soften. Then shower him with understanding and peace.

- End with a prayer of goodwill, something like this: "May the anger I have felt serve to relieve someone else of having to feel anger. May this experience help to lessen the amount of anger in the world, and lessen the power of anger over all people."

In order to understand the suffering that anger produces In countless human beings, we must set aside our personal response to it long enough to feel and understand the whole phenomenon more clearly. When we do this, anger no longer controls us as it once did, because we see many of the falsehoods involved and the ways we have tricked ourselves into acting blindly or hysterically. This practice can be a giant step toward true freedom.

A Mensch Is a Mensch, Big or Small

The biggest part of my life right now is raising my kids. But when I look around at children of various ages from perfectly decent parents, I see so many who are frightened, or feel inadequate or depressed, or seem very angry. I begin to wonder, what are good parents missing about proper child-raising? Why is it so hard for our kids to be happy?

What is our view of priorities for a child's life? Do we even have a view? Have we looked at child-raising from any perspective broader than our own narrow cultural milieu? In ancient Hindu society, for example, even the most privileged kids, the children of kings and emperors, were sent at a very young age into the forest ashrams of rugged sages, living there for several years without any luxuries, to learn true unselfishness by serving the sage. In return, they were taught the values of their religion, became proficient in forest living, and developed patience and physical hardiness.

In other traditional cultures too, childhood was mainly about learning those same three things:

- Values
- Skills
- Self-discipline

Children must learn the *values* of their people so they can become decent members of the social order. They must learn a variety of practical *skills* so they can be productive and self-supporting. They must learn the *self-discipline* to get them through life's inevitable setbacks. These character traits give children a sense of connection to others, a sense of their place in the great scheme of life, and a sense of responsibility to the common good. They give children the self-respect and confidence essential to true happiness.

How many of these three qualities do modern children learn? In our era, values, skills, and self-discipline have taken quite a beating. Childhood is geared around either self-centered fun and irresponsibility or relentless pressure to excel academically (or athletically) to ensure a secure personal future. Either way, our children are extraordinarily insulated and separated from values, skills, and self-discipline relating to the common good. I believe this is a big reason why modern American kids are so lost and angry.

People of every age need to feel useful, and need to be skilled at something. People need a reason to tune in to what's going on. We can't just expect them to reach a certain age and then suddenly take responsibility. In order to take responsibility, they must first care about life, about the world. And in our current fashion of child-raising, they have not been learning how to care about anything deeper than their own immediate sense gratification or plans for their own future.

Many kids these days have only a vague impression of what their parents do for a living. The kids themselves have no direct role in their family's daily needs or maintenance. Many families rarely eat a meal together anymore. Siblings are often not required to rely on each other or support each other. Even educated, liberal parents sometimes boast that they do not intend to teach their children religious or moral values, but will "allow them to decide for themselves" what they wish to believe in. From any traditional perspective, this is more than grossly misguided parenting; it is cultural suicide.

Our children start out physically healthier and intellectually sharper than ever before. With such fantastic potential, we should be able to help mold them into radiantly happy and helpful human beings! We certainly love them enough to do it; we have simply lost our link with classic parenting. While our society and our school systems are clearly in a period of upheaval and confusion, we need to take more time and care than ever to guide our children through such turbulent straits.

The way children move through childhood and adolescence is not random. If we put the time in, expand our views, and reassess the priorities of childhood, our kids will be fine human beings. If we do not require children to be responsible, skilled, and needed, if we create no meaningful initiations from one stage of childhood to another, then children tend to form their own groups to accomplish those basic human needs. They may form social cliques in which they can experience initiation, define their identity and value to the others, pledge their loyalty, and learn the skills relevant to that group—even if the cliques are gangs, and the relevant skills happen to involve a credit card to pick a lock, or a complex set of hand signals, or a secret language that adults won't understand.

Helena Norberg-Hodge is a European woman who spent many years living in the tiny Himalayan region of Ladakh. In her insightful book, *Ancient Futures: Learning from Ladakh,* she points out that before our modern Western educational system came to that area, the society was basically a whole nation of *menschen*. (*Mensch* is Yiddish for "a real person," someone who is reliable and handy to have around.) Children grew up learning their society's Buddhist values of compassion, nonviolence, and harmony, and virtually every boy and girl, by the time they reached adolescence, knew how to grow and prepare food, mend clothes, care for animals, build houses, construct complex irrigation systems. In short, Ladakhi youngsters naturally became moral, capable, and happy young adults.

Then "progress" came. Thousands of children were removed from their villages, crammed into classrooms to memorize facts and recite their times tables. They no longer learned from their parents, aunts, uncles, grandparents; they no longer shared the responsibility of food production, warmth, shelter, child care; they had a more "privileged" childhood, like that of American children, not needing to contribute to their family's daily welfare. But as Ms. Hodge explains, when their education was finished and they returned to their villages, they were essentially useless. They had been cut off from the wealth of values, skills, and self-discipline that had made the Ladakhis a happy people for hundreds of years. Today, many of those children have migrated to the larger cities around India or Nepal, becoming prostitutes or drug abusers or apathetic minimum-wage workers. It's a very sad situation, similar to the devastation of the Native American cultures in the United States.

CUTTING OUT THE OLD AND THE YOUNG

On the other end of the age spectrum we see some of the same attitudes. Terms like "retirement community" and "assisted living" sound positive and even make sense in some ways, but let's face it: as a society, we seem to have concluded that old people have no usefulness in the family or community and that it is inconvenient to keep them around. They slow us down; they take up our time. We see no importance in children spending significant time with their grandparents or vice versa.

In order to feel connected to life, we must contribute something positive toward the common good. Children and elderly people are no exception. By sheltering children from responsibility and putting the elderly out to pasture, we have unwittingly created an angry, aimless younger generation and a lonely, undervalued older generation.

Many modern Americans assume this is simply what it means to be young or to be old. But anyone who has traveled in other cultures knows this is not true. Children can be happy, respectful, and capable. The elderly can be peaceful, wise, venerated. People of several generations can live together joyfully under one roof.

Life is a holy and mysterious process all the way through. There are wonders and challenges in every stage of life. Each stage is worthy of equal respect. Each stage requires values, skill, and self-discipline. And in every stage, we need each other in order to be naturally, happily complete. We need young, middle-aged, and old people around us, not just others our own age. We are ever and always part of each other. We either walk into heaven on earth arm in arm, or we never find the gate.

A Practice: TAKING INVENTORY

At this moment, there are many millions of angry young people and lonely old people. The situation won't turn around overnight. But each one of us can begin the process of turning it around by sizing up our own lives with respect to values, skills, and self-discipline, and doing whatever we need to do in order to bring those qualities up to our liking. We can gradually chip away at the age-denying, death-denying nature of modern life.

- For example, if you dye your hair to look younger, please stop! Gray hair is beautiful. White hair is beautiful. It is beautiful to look our age. If anyone asks your age, please do not stammer or lie or joke. Children see us all trying to look like twenty-five-year-olds, yet twenty-five-year-olds are not especially happy themselves. What a dismal catch-22. They need to see us older people being happy with who we are.

- Look at how you treat your children and elders and see whether you are allowing them their own areas of usefulness and responsibility toward the family's welfare. In what nonartificial ways might you learn to rely a little more on each other?

- Steadily dismantle every notion you have imbibed that a meaningful life is about money, accomplishments, prestige, or recreation, and cease to pass such notions on to your kids. Make it almost like a family game, to notice and discuss commercials, articles, shows, books, and advertisements that reinforce such wrong

views. Get your kids used to probing past the surface
a little.

- Develop common sense and basic skills, at any age,
  so that you become more self-reliant and adaptable to
  changing circumstances. Learn how to change a flat
  tire or bake a delicious loaf of bread (see the following
  chapter, Fix Your La-Z-Boy, for more on this subject).
- Size up your way of talking and make sure that you
  say what you mean and mean what you say—no hidden agendas or broken promises to others or yourself.
- Spend time in nature with no ifs, ands, or buts—and
  without taking a cell phone with you! And if your kids
  don't want to go, tell them they have to because you
  feel it's important. They won't curl up and die if they
  see that you mean it.

Values, skills, and self-discipline make for a more enjoyable
experience of living, more self-respect and confidence and
friendliness to others. We can put ourselves and our kids and
our elders back on this time-honored path to freedom and see
how it begins to affect the folks next door and down the block.
Everyone wants to feel more hopeful these days. A humble,
personal step in the right direction is a contribution to the
whole world, a wonderful way to further a life of service.

Fix Your La-Z-Boy

I usually hire people to do the small tasks that need to be taken care of. I have the money, and I'd rather spend my time on more enjoyable things than fixing the sink or painting the porch. Won't that give me more time for a meaningful life?

The Buddha once listed fifteen qualities that are essential for a meaningful life. At the very top of the list was "To be able": to be a capable person, to have a variety of skills that come in handy that give us self-respect and provide various honorable ways to make a living.

That wasn't just conceptual advice from the Buddha, it was his recognition that human beings have an inherent need to be capable. That doesn't mean that each of us must be able to do everything, but how did it come about that millions of people in our modern society reach adulthood having almost no practical skills?

It is a big mistake to assume that this issue refers mostly to underprivileged kids needing a better education. I was an honors student all through school, yet I never picked up a hammer or grew a tomato or fixed a flat tire until adulthood. I was smart academically, but I felt incompetent and useless outside of school. Most kids these days of every socioeconomic group seem to feel the same way, and many of them feel incompetent and useless inside of school as well.

As I mentioned in the preceding chapter, the Jewish culture has a well-known word for a capable person: mensch. A mensch is someone to whom you can loan your car without worrying about it; someone who can figure out how to get the crumbly piece of toast out of the toaster without electrocuting anybody; someone you would like to work with, or have next to you in a fire, or a stuck elevator, or an earthquake or hurricane.

What does it take to be able, or to be a mensch? In modern times, we tend to condescend toward those with practical and hands-on capability. I was always told that with my brains, I would be able to hire a "blue-collar" person to fix things or build things, no need to dirty my own hands with such trifles. Yet my deepest and most joyful education has been learning how to build my own home, plow the land, grow food, fix my recliner without sending it back to La-Z-Boy. But I had to learn all these things on my own, as an adult. Why?

John Taylor Gatto, a former New York City public school teacher who has become one of the most outspoken whistleblowers on the nation's school system, points out that schools merely school, they do not provide an education. I love the passionate way Gatto put it in an interview:

> Are you a schoolteacher? Can you build a house or a boat? Can you grow food, make your own clothing, dig a well, sing a song (your own song, that is), make your own children happy, weave a whole life from the everyday world around you? No? You say you can't? Then listen to me, you have no business with my kid.

In his first book, *Dumbing Us Down,* Gatto provides compelling evidence that not only does our modern school system fail to produce capable and happy young adults, but that it actually strips students of their capacity for original or creative thinking and contributes to learning disabilities. Grouping children solely in their own age groups despite differences in natural interest or intelligence, ringing a bell every forty-five minutes to prevent children from delving deeply into any subject, herding them through drab hallways and classrooms regardless of the beautiful weather outside—what are we thinking? How does a mensch arise from that sort of indoctrination? Gatto continues,

> In centuries past, the time of a child and adolescent would be occupied in real work, real charity, real adventures, and the real search for mentors who might teach what one really wanted to learn. A great deal of time was spent in community pursuits, practicing affection, meeting and studying every level of the community, learning how to make a home, and dozens of other tasks necessary to becoming a whole man or woman.

We have lost many of those resources and opportunities, so we must make up for that loss by taking matters into our own hands, literally. If we become "neo-menschen" ourselves, our kids may be able to follow a well-rounded and joyfully capable path a little earlier than we did.

Merely by paying attention to how things are put together, or asking a little advice from various tradespeople, or getting the right reference manual, a whole world of self-reliance opened up to me that had been shrouded in an unapproachable mystique all my life. I would go so far as to say that something inside me was not complete until I became handier.

In fact, I struggled with my first book, *We're All Doing Time,* for nearly seven years, concluding that I'd never be able to finish it. Then I spent a year building my house. It was daunting, almost overwhelming, because I had never built so much as a Popsicle-stick house before. I was sure I couldn't become a genuine "blue-collar guy" who understood framing, plumbing, wiring, and so forth.

I approached the whole formidable task with fear and loathing, my sole motivation being to avoid having a mortgage. But the building process itself worked on me in surprising ways. After three months, when the well was dug and the rough framing was nearly done, I was beginning to feel a little less like a fraud, and could hardly wait to get out there every day. Around that time, Sita joined me in the daily work routine, which put me in the foreman role, and I began to see that actually I had already learned quite a bit, and I was doing all right. Sita brought an aesthetic dimension to the project that made the ongoing work even more enjoyable, because we could see beauty arise as well as shelter.

But at times I still felt overwhelmed and was afraid that I had bitten off much more than I could chew. That's when a Buddhist monk came to live with us for several months. He had just returned from eight years in forest monasteries in Thailand. One night at dinner, while I was bellyaching about how daunting it was to build a house, he finally had enough and said, "You know, Bo, most of the people in the world build their own homes, and they do it in about a week."

It's difficult to explain how deep an effect that one impatient sentence had on me. It somehow tore through many layers of mystique, self-doubt, conceit, and opened my eyes to the fact that what I was doing was not so special, not so extraordinary. In fact, it was a very basic and common thing to do. I was providing shelter for my family. Big deal. So long as I didn't make a stupid mistake on any particular day and leave it unfixed, then I would not have a stupid mistake in the eventual house. All the mystique was instantaneously gone forever.

For one full school year, Sita and I dropped Josh off at school, went to work on the house, picked him up in the afternoons, and went home to do our prison work in the evenings. When the house was done, I had become a man. And then *We're All Doing Time* fell into place. How could I find it impossible to finish a book when I had just succeeded in building an entire house?

JOSH'S TWO COMPLAINTS

In 1991, Sita and I celebrated our twenty-fifth wedding anniversary by spending the day with Josh in a remote spot at the bottom of the Rio Grande Gorge in northern New Mexico. The three of us took the opportunity to clean out old baggage with each other, air any secrets, deepen our sense of love and connection and loyalty to each other. Josh was twenty years old at the time.

At one point during the day, I asked Josh if there was any way we had let him down as parents. After reflection, he said there were actually two ways. "First of all, whenever something was hard for me to do, you guys helped me so much that I didn't develop much self-discipline. That hurt me a lot when I lived in L.A., because I had to develop all my discipline on my own. You didn't help me become very tough or adaptable.

"The second thing is, Dad, do you remember when I was fourteen and I told you that when I finished high school I wanted to go out to L.A. to be an actor instead of going to college?" I told him I remembered, and he continued.

"Well, you said that I would have your blessing on one condition: that by the time I left home, I was a skilled carpenter. That way, whether I succeeded in my acting career or not, I would still be able to make a good living and feel the satisfaction of working with my hands."

Once again, I told him I remembered. Then Josh said, "But you didn't make me do it. You didn't force me to become a good carpenter, and you gave me your blessing anyway. You should have stuck by your word."

I protested, "But I tried! I built five buildings between the time you were fourteen and the time you left home, and I tried to get you to help me on every one of them. It was like pulling teeth to get you to help. So I gave up. I didn't want to force you."

Josh replied, "That's exactly what I mean: You should have forced me. You were the parent and I was the kid. You set a condition for your blessing and then you didn't make me live up to it. You should have made me become a good carpenter whether I liked it or not."

He was right. In our family, a parent's blessing means something. If I had continued to make it clear to Josh that he would be leaving home without my blessing at age eighteen, he would have become a proficient carpenter even if he didn't enjoy it. And here he was, as an adult, telling us that kids don't really want to be so self-determining. They want to be needed and involved and held accountable, even though they may resist it at the time.

My original parental instinct had been correct: even by

age twenty, Josh wished he were a good carpenter. I had gotten caught in the easy way out rather than the right way. Our children may fuss and fume, but on the whole, they do not seem to be either benefited or grateful for the radical degree of autonomy many of us grant them, especially, I think, when we parents act out of weakness rather than deliberate philosophy.

Sita and I asked Josh for forgiveness on both counts. He asked for ours as well, for testing our failings as he had. It was a great day—a renewal of deep affection, commitment, and trust. I recommend such an occasional event to any family.

These family stories are not unusual. Most Americans grow up long on concepts and short on skills. We are some of the most incompetent adults on the planet when the lights go out or the earth quakes or a hurricane roars through. And that means that something deep within us is going to feel dissatisfied or incomplete, because human beings have a need to be capable and adaptive. That's part of a meaningful life.

A Practice: WORKING WITH YOUR HANDS

Most of us consider ourselves klutzes, so we give up without even considering whether we might enjoy fixing a household problem ourselves. But these days, how-to advice is free for the asking, all over the place.

A short while ago my shower broke. Knowing how much plumbers charge, I felt compelled to at least give it a try, even though plumbing is not my forte. In my first phone call to Home

Depot, my description narrowed the problem to a broken "diverter stem." This is the gadget that switches the water flow back and forth between the bathtub and the shower.

My next question was, "Is this fairly straightforward, or am I going to be sorry I tried doing this myself?" The clerk said it really wasn't too big a deal, Home Depot had the replacement parts, and to remember to turn off the water supply to the house before trying to take the old one off.

Buying the new part and examining it closely is very helpful before removing the old part. You get to understand how it's made, how many pieces it comprises, whether there are any washers that may fall off. The old part on my shower was a little rusty and needed a few sprays of Liquid Wrench before it would come free with a vise grips, but all in all, the actual repair took about a half hour and cost about $10. How much would a plumber have charged? And although I don't especially enjoy plumbing, I do enjoy victory!

There are so many things in our modern life we don't know how to do, nor are we teaching our children how to fix or build things. I heard of a young man who needed his parents to accompany him when he first went away to college across the country. Why? Because he couldn't hang his own bulletin board, or do a load of laundry, or put together a desk. Were his parents being kind by never teaching him how to be able to do such ordinary tasks?

Take a look at the following list and try to learn how to deal with at least a couple of these everyday situations. Better yet, tackle one or more of these with your child and see how gleeful a simple repair can become. For the most part, like a drunk who has forgotten what being sober feels like, we modern people have become so narrowly specialized, we have forgotten the intrinsic satisfaction of being well-rounded and handy.

• **Household**

Wire a lamp

Use a jigsaw

Rehang a window

Sew curtains

Change the fan belt in the dryer

Frame a picture

Fix a leaky faucet

Replace a water heater

Install a new toilet

Bake bread

• **Outdoor**

Fix a flat tire

Cut your own firewood

Tune up the lawn mower

Chop down a dead tree

Grow a vegetable garden

Build a fence

Repair a roof

Repaint the chimney

• **Office**

Change a computer card

Service the copy machine

Change the toner in the printer

Put together a bookcase

Hang shelves

Change a fluorescent lightbulb

Install new software

Install a modem

Success by Failure

How can I commit myself to any sort of service when my own life is a constant struggle marked by failures, big and small? If I don't feel like a success, how can I help others be successful?

What a vicious circle we can put ourselves in: we have come to accept a notion of "fix me first," when part of the essential fixing we all need is to be compassionately involved with others. Life does not happen sequentially; it comes at us from many directions at once. Those of us who delay helping others until we are happy enough, or rich enough, or peaceful enough, never seem to get around to it. Besides, we miss the point: our struggles are part of our common humanity, part of our mutually helpful link with others.

Even personal failure or tragedy can be a profound springboard into deeper levels of our most important virtues such as humility and commitment. In the spiritual life, it is never too early, never too late, and never a bad time to turn things around. Once we do, we will see that all those very things we considered to be our worst failures turn out to have been the very building blocks of our compassion and humility.

Many of us consider large parts of our lives to be miserable failures. Great! We're halfway there. We're "poor in Spirit." The very first of the beatitudes Jesus preached from the mountain was "Blessed are the poor in Spirit, for theirs is the Kingdom of Heaven."

I love the story of Simon Peter in the New Testament. He was the boldest and bravest of all the disciples, a coarse, no-nonsense fisherman, and fiercely loyal to Jesus. When Jesus asked all the apostles, "How do you see me?" Peter was the only one who had the guts to say, "I see you as the Messiah, the Son of the Living God." When Jesus walked on water toward the boat carrying his disciples, Peter was the only one who also took a few steps on the water. But Peter lacked humility. He thought he could never fall prey to weakness like you or me. He was special.

In the Garden of Gethsemane, Jesus hinted that there would be some trouble. Peter's response: "Well, even if the others run away, I will never leave you, Lord; I will never betray you." Jesus said, "Oh, Peter, you're just like all the rest." Peter's reply: "Lord, I will not betray you. I would give my life for you!" Jesus said, "Peter, before the cock crows tomorrow morning, you will deny three times that you ever even knew me."

Not Peter. Tough guy. Not a coward. *Jesus is wrong this time. I'll prove it to him.*

Peter must have found it horrific and astonishing as he saw himself betray and deny Jesus like a common coward later that night. No excuses, no way around it. I'm sure the temptation to turn tail and never show his face again, or even to commit suicide, as Judas did, must have been almost overwhelming. He lied. He chickened out. He betrayed Jesus. He failed miserably to be a decent human being. And that terrible, inexcusable failure is precisely what finally made Peter ready to be the rock of the church.

Jesus knew that Peter lacked humility. How could Peter show you or me the way to Christ if he could not identify with our shame and regrets, our weaknesses and inadequacies? So, Peter's most miserable worldly failure led to his greatest spiritual success. That's what it took to humble his pride.

Sita and I once entertained for a few days a family guest who was very bubbly, talkative, and extroverted. The day she left was the same day we expected the arrival of another friend, someone we had never met in person but had known for the whole ten years he had spent in prison for murder. Our correspondence and books and tapes had helped him to change his life, and now that he had been released from prison, coming to meet us took on the importance for him of a holy pilgrimage.

Our family member left early in the morning, and then Sita and I went about our morning meditation practice. Our minds were noisy, unfocused from several days of boisterousness. We commented to each other that we wished we could change our consciousness for our next visitor, who was definitely coming to meet us as spiritual elders, not good-time hosts. We said a little prayer asking to feel humbler and quieter by the time of his arrival.

Soon we went for our daily hike in the forest, and about a half mile into the woods we got into an intense argument over something that neither of us has the vaguest memory of today. We shouted and screamed at each other, defiling the beauty of nature, and confusing the hell out of ourselves. We then felt doubly sickened by the thought of our visitor's arrival in just a few more hours. We headed back home in tense silence, lit the candles on our altar, and sat down on our cushions. Within a minute, I heard a little voice say inside me, "Feel humbled and quieted yet?"

I looked over at Sita, who was getting the same message. We had indeed both gotten all the boisterousness knocked out of us through shame and humiliation. By the time our prison friend arrived that afternoon, we were softer and quieter than we had been in a long time.

Peter the Apostle probably prayed for humility. His prayer was answered through his betrayal of Jesus. Sita's and my prayers were answered by our descent into temporary insanity with each other. But the prayers were answered. Should we be fussy about God's methods?

You and I have failed many times. We have let people down. We have been dishonest, cowardly, mean. We have hurt ourselves and others. If we allow our failures to open us up instead of shut us down, if we allow them to humble us instead of defeat us, then every lousy thing we have ever done can be turned into the very foundation of our devotion and compassion. Every human being contains the highest of the high and lowest of the low. We have no right to look down on anyone, no matter what he or she has done. Peter must have been so ashamed and humiliated, he probably never wanted to show his face again. But he did. He came down from his lofty perch. He didn't quit or run away. He didn't try to forget all about it. He accepted his flawed nature, opened his heart, and moved forward a quieter, gentler man who knew he indeed was "just like all the rest." He could then become the saint we are all destined to become.

PUTTING OUR FAILURES TO GOOD USE

All of us deal with many people very day. Everyone we meet hopes we will be kind and humble and unselfish. They don't care where we learned it. They don't care whether it came easy or hard, through failures or successes. If the guy next to you starts choking, he doesn't care where or how you learned the Heimlich maneuver, he just hopes you use it!

Without Peter's failure, there may not have been a Christian church. Without my failures, there certainly wouldn't have been a Human Kindness Foundation or a Prison-Ashram Project. What would your life be like without your failures? Do you accept them as much as your successes?

One thing we can begin taking for granted is that every person we meet who seems to have courage, dignity, compassion, and humility has experienced failure and weakness and shame. Our spiritual success rests not on whether we have failed, but only on what we are willing to do with our failures.

We must be careful of how we regard success. Gandhi said there are many things he would die for, but nothing he would kill for. In other words, be willing to stand up for what is right at any cost, but we must not do what we think is wrong even if the greatest job, the biggest promotion, the most money in the world is dangled in front of us.

If we want to be a spiritual success, we must always have the strength to walk away from temptation. Most of us don't want to hear this. We especially don't want our kids to hear this, because it is natural as parents to want our kids to have security, comfort, and some conceptual spirituality.

But concepts of spirituality are not real spirituality. Or as Sufi Sam once said, "Concepts of God have to do with concepts, not with God." We can't have everything. Real spirituality is not secure in any worldly sense; it is not safe, and not always comfortable. How many of us want to be reminded that, according to the Bible, "the love of money is the root of all kinds of evil" (1 Timothy 6:10)? How many of us want to be reminded to keep the sick, the poor, the oppressed in our hearts all through the day? These are the tenets of spirituality. Always have been, always will be. In one of his classic meditations, the Roman Emperor Marcus Aurelius writes, "Let your one delight and refreshment be to pass from one service to the community to another, with God ever in mind." These are the principles of true success, which paradoxically blooms from our brokenness and openness to each other, not from our egocentric conquests or achievements.

A *Practice*: A DAY OF SILENCE

Occasional periods of silence are recommended by every wisdom tradition. Modern life can be extremely noisy, and this constant noise can keep us from seeing ourselves as honestly or clearly as we may like. Sita and I have found great value in many periods of silence. For several years, each of us spent one day a week in silence. At various times, we have spent longer periods as well, like my own two-month silent retreat in 1991. At Kindness House, where we live now, there is often one person or another in silence on any given day. We find that the entire community is benefited and quieted down at least a little bit when one of us is practicing silence. It feels very civilized.

There are two main types of the practice of silence, both of which are valuable in different ways. In either case, determine in advance what you mean by a "day" so there is no potential for confusion. Some people around here spend a day of silence until dinner, others from the time they get up one morning until the time they get up the next morning, still others from sundown to sundown.

1. *Silence in an otherwise normal day*

   Practicing silence in an otherwise normal day can provide us with insight into the nature of our speech patterns. It also shows us that the world gets along quite well without our two cents' worth, and usually inspires us to try to speak a little bit less when we do resume speaking.

   • The best way to prepare for this practice of silence is to let your close associates, especially family and bosses, know about it in advance. Then print a little card simply saying something like, "I'm practicing a day of silence." You can choose to explain more, or to add, "Thanks for your understanding," but keep it brief and don't worry too much about whether people will understand. It's great if they do, but some will not, and may make a joke of it or even resent you for it. Allow them the dignity of their own spiritual challenges. All you're doing is taking a day of silence. Keep it simple and unpretentious.

   • Keep a notepad and pencil handy, but clarify to yourself in advance what sorts of encounters you may need to participate in by writing such notes. In general, you do not need to join in on social or personal discussions. That's part of what you are taking a break from. Work-related matters are different. Even there, be as brief as possible and true to your intent of disengaging yourself from all but the most necessary matters of communication. You may want a second prepared card that reads, "Can I discuss this with you tomorrow?"

- At mealtimes, smile a lot if you need to reassure your companions that you are present with them and fully aware and friendly. You may be surprised at how much effect one silent person can have on a table full of conversation—especially when conversation turns to gossip or backbiting. In a way, your silent witness may help others better hear what they sound like.

2. *Silent retreat day*

The other way of practicing silence is to retreat from all your normal activities and from the presence of others to the greatest degree possible. If you can't go to a cabin in the woods or some other isolated place, you may want to turn off the ringers on your phones, pull down the shades, and simply spend the day in your home or even in your bedroom. Or you can make a prior agreement with your family or roommates so that they will not find it rude or strange to see you around the house or yard but ignoring them on that day.

However you arrange it, here are a few tips to get the most out of a day of silent retreat:

- Plan your meals in advance, and plan for only about half of what you may normally eat. This will help you be quieter. Simple foods, maybe even avoiding anything that needs to be cooked or fussed over, are best. I usually take a heel of bread and a piece or two of fruit in with me.

- Do not spend a lot of the day reading. If you choose to read at all, plan it in advance and limit it to brief spiritual writings that may help you to work with silence.
- Do not listen to music or watch television.
- Try to spend some time in nature, just listening and observing. If you have no access to the great outdoors, then at least spend time watching the sky and all its changes.
- Try not to let your thoughts dominate the day. The best way to do this is to focus on perceptions of the senses—seeing, listening, touching, smelling, tasting, chewing, walking. Pay attention "outside" the mind by keeping your attention on the present moment.
- Breathe. Slow breaths, deep breaths can help quiet the mind and body. Make friends with your breath while you are in silence.

Honest Truth and Honest Fiction

———————— 🌿 ————————

I've been taught all my life to trust my own feelings, that they won't steer me wrong. As long as I'm honest with myself, my life will proceed as it should. But my honesty and my husband's honesty, my honesty and my friend's honesty, clash a lot. How can I live in community with others and still be true to myself?

Sita may honestly believe I am the handsomest man in the world. That doesn't make it objectively true. Honesty and truth are only identical in a fully enlightened sage. While self-honesty is crucial to a good life, there are many times when it is wise to trust others more than we trust ourselves, times when our spouse or friends or family can see our blind spots and rationalizations more clearly than we can. Rather than defending "your truth" against input from others, you can grow much faster by practicing what Thich Nhat Hanh calls "deep listening"—holding your personal honesty up to the light of a possibly more objective truth when appropriate.

One of the first residents of Kindness House was a man named Norman who had served twenty-two years in prison for a terrible double murder he had committed at the age of eighteen. Norman began to take stock of his life in his twenties, and gradually took responsibility for educating himself, getting clean and sober (a harder task in prison than you may suspect), and participating in virtually every positive program his prison had to offer. By the time we met him in his late thirties, he was head of his prison chapter of the NAACP and a genuinely compassionate person. He had made the Big Change. He was no longer dangerous, no longer the dysfunctional, cocaine-crazed killer he had once been.

During his first month in our community, at one of our weekly tunings (house meetings), Norman looked bothered and was acting sullen. I asked him what was wrong, and at first he refused to say anything other than "Nothing; don't worry about it." The group reminded him that our tunings were a time of honesty and, if necessary, a time of clearing the air with another person. Norman finally mumbled, "I saw the look on Bo's face when he walked through the warehouse this morning and found me talking to Sita alone."

I had no memory of seeing Sita and Norman talking in the warehouse that day. I said, "What look are you talking about, Norman?" Looking down at the floor, he said tersely, "You know exactly what I'm talking about." I replied, a little tersely myself, "No, I don't know what you're talking about. What look do you think you saw on my face?" Still not able to look at me, Norman said, "You didn't like your wife being alone with a black man."

I said, "Norman, first of all, I didn't even notice you and Sita when I walked through the warehouse. Second of all, I don't have a problem with a black man being alone with my wife."

With a hard, piercing look of total confidence and conviction, for the first time Norman looked straight into my eyes: "I know what I saw," he said. I met his gaze with equal steeliness, and said: "But what you saw was not the truth."

I had to stare him down before he was willing to question his "honest" perception.

This story is worth reflection because, like Norman, we have all been influenced by a contemporary psychological principle that goes something like this:

> Trust your own truth. If it's true for you, then it doesn't matter whether it is true for others. Be true to yourself.

This bespeaks a very dangerous confusion between honesty and truth, and an equally dangerous implication that truth is always relative. I had no doubts about Norman's honesty. He honestly believed I had a problem with his being alone with Sita. But it was not true. It wasn't just "not true for me," it was not true for Norman either. It was not true, period.

When we make self-honesty identical to objective truth, we become rigid and unquestioning of our own perceptions—as many modern people indeed seem to be doing. Norman had taken psychological courses in prison, and they had encouraged him to be honest about his feelings. That is important, of course. But they did not provide the balance of making sure he understood that his feelings are not always in line with reality. That is a dangerous oversight.

Another resident of Kindness House, who had spent ten years in prison for murder, had a hard time following house rules and going along with the community's ways of doing things. When chided, Terry always responded, "I have to do what that little voice inside tells me to do. Anytime I have not followed it, I have gotten in trouble." I often reasoned with Terry that the little voice of self-protection and autonomy he resorted to was probably essential in the brutal prison environment where he had to survive against many odds, but now he was in a new environment, and here, that same little voice was actually a major hindrance to his growth. He always just smiled and said, "I know what I need to do."

Mother Meera, a silent Indian holy woman who lives in Germany, commented specifically on this issue. She wrote, "I recommend that people neither pay attention to nor determine their actions on the basis of such voices, as it is difficult to tell where these voices come from."

I know another convict whose behavior points out the most perilous and twisted edge of this honesty-versus-truth question. Bobby got out of a mental hospital a few years ago and showed up at the home of his psychiatrist, who he honestly thought was attracted to him. She came to the door and told him quite bluntly that it was inappropriate for him to have come to her house. She did not want to deal with him at that time. Bobby became abusive, and the door was shut in his face. From her lawn, he started yelling, "I know what your game is here! You want me to rough you up. You want me to break your door down. You're trying to get me to be violent. That's what turns you on!" Obviously, Bobby was soon back in custody. Bobby told me this story himself, and he was being honest about his feelings at the time. He couldn't see it any other way.

Maybe few of us are so erroneous in our self-honesty as Bobby. But you and I may fall into a dozen minor traps every day over the same confusion between emotional honesty and objective truth.

Part of the problem is that pop psychology encourages us

to believe in ourselves in a way which may inadvertently associate all self-doubt with failure. But questioning our feelings or motives is not neurotic or flawed. It does not mean we don't believe in ourselves. It is actually a healthy part of the process of integrating our personal perceptions into the world around us. Our feelings are complex varmints that are colored by desires, fears, moods, upbringing, biological cycles, and countless other factors. One of the prime purposes of a wholesome lifestyle, daily spiritual practice, and a caring community is to bring our feelings more in line with reality. To assume they start out that way is crazy.

If our honest feelings are unreliable at best and catastrophic at worst, then how does God guide us? Usually by intuition. And intuition is rarely, if ever, accompanied by certainty. The experience in intuition is more like a hunch, a best guess, a subtle feeling making us lean toward one thing or another without really being sure of why. Intuition is humble and open to other influences. As we strengthen our intuition, the self-confidence we develop is soft and quiet, not assertive or rigid. It's more of a whole-bodied realization that something or other beckons us.

God-realization does not come about merely by a surface understanding of "ceasing to judge myself harshly," or "always accepting the truth of my feelings." The spiritual awakening we all yearn for is much grander and more earthshaking than that, thank God!

A Practice: TALKING CIRCLE—OPENING HONESTY TO TRUTH

Have a few friends, family members, or colleagues read this chapter and then convene a focused discussion on whatever questions of honesty versus truth seem relevant for the people involved.

- *Self-perception* is always an interesting area to explore. Let's say I claim to be cutting down on workaholism. I say to the talking circle, "I feel I am cutting down on workaholism, and I honestly feel I'm making big strides toward being more relaxed and so forth. From your perception, how do you think I am doing? Am I fooling myself?"

The commitment from members of your circle will be not to hedge in their responses, but to truly give you the benefit of their perspective, even if it is a little uncomfortable to express. This isn't like the old sixties game called Group Therapy, where you may then come under attack; this is very different. A talking circle is a sacred trust of goodwill and fellowship. You must be able to assume that all the members of the group sincerely wish to support each other's growth. That's the key to swallowing the occasionally bitter pill you are handed by the group.

For example, our board of directors' meetings are essentially talking circles. At the 1997 circle it was decided that I should cut back my schedule a little and take more time to rest. When our 1998 meeting convened, the minutes from 1997 were read and reviewed. I said I felt pretty good about having heeded that suggestion, and then my son took the floor and rattled off about a half dozen ways I still wasn't giving my body the attention it needed at my age. He wasn't attacking or accusing me, he was sharing his loving concern that I was fooling myself. That's how a talking circle works.

Similar questions can be asked regarding diet and nutrition, patterns of speech such as dirty jokes or impatient responses, or other egotistic behaviors. A musician friend of mine, a talented folksinger and guitarist, visits Kindness House often, and plays music with us or for us. He told me privately that he feels no ego involvement or vanity connected with performing; he feels he is long past that. Based on several years' experience of his visits to our community, I said, "Why don't you ask all the members of this community how they feel about that, because my hunch is that every one of them would say that you are very talented and enjoyable to listen to, and that you are also extremely ego-involved with your talents. Could they all be wrong?"

Of course, theoretically they could all indeed be wrong. But most of the time, when the people who know us and love us speak in one voice about how we come across to them, we need to listen and reflect. What self-perceptions might you want to bounce off of your family, friends, co-workers, or even your boss? It could be very interesting!

- *Perception of others* is another good reality check for a talking circle every now and then, especially when you feel a conflict because of it. Like Norman's perception of my discomfort over him talking with Sita, sometimes these honest but mistaken feelings can seriously damage our relationships with others. And worst of all, the other person may have no idea what's going on. The longer we hold on to our incorrect notions, the less we question them, and they tend to become a hidden "fact" that we assume the other knows as well. Yet the whole tempest may be solely in our own minds.

- *Perception of the world* is another valuable reality check for a talking circle. My mother, who generally watches every news show and TV magazine show from early morning until late at night, has a pretty jaundiced view of how the world is doing. My sister-in-law, who works with ghetto kids and sees lives changing one at a time and is too busy to watch the news, is much more upbeat. Both views, of course, are only partial views, seen from their own range of observations. It's useful to balance our views by bouncing them off of our friends and colleagues. In many ways, the world is indeed in terrible shape, and it is important to be aware of that. And in many ways, people are absolutely wonderful and courageous and inspiring, and it is essential to be aware of that as well.

A few things distinguish a talking circle from a casual conversation:

- One person speaks at a time. Do not cut anyone off.
- Practice what Thich Nhat Hanh calls "deep listening" to each speaker. This means to feel what the speaker feels, from his or her point of view, before you compare or contrast it with your own view. This is an extremely valuable skill to develop.
- Set a time limit for the talking circle. This helps everyone maintain good energy and commitment, without worrying that it'll go on forever if you all decide to be really honest with each other.

- Being aired and heard is more important than getting every issue resolved. There may be many things that take time to reflect on.
- It's good to end a talking circle with some sort of acknowledgment of gratitude and goodwill, even if the meeting raised some conflicts.

A Time to Speak

❧

In changing my attitude to try to be more loving toward people I encounter, I'm sometimes confused. Am I supposed to give them what they want or what I think they need? And who am I to judge them?

There is a time for everything, and a season for every activity under Heaven. . . .

A time to be silent and a time to speak . . .
—Ecclesiastes 3:1–37

An issue related to the distinction between honesty and truth is the distinction between judging and discernment. I don't think a day goes by that I don't hear someone say, "Well, I don't want to judge . . . ," or "Well, I'm probably being judgmental . . ." These are among the most constant buzz-phrases of our time. But have we a clear idea what we're saying?

It is not judgmental to hold a different philosophy. It is not judgmental to strongly disagree with a friend or to exhort others to change their minds or their behavior when we think they may bring harm to themselves or someone else. It is not judgmental to offer good-faith critiques of books, movies, lectures, or workshops. It is absolutely not judgmental to have a huge influence in the morals and philosophies of our own children. This is all legitimate and important human conduct.

In recent times, we have isolated and alienated ourselves from each other to an alarming degree by misunderstanding the difference between judging and discerning. We have developed an exaggerated "hands-off" ethic from each other's opinions and behavior, which will definitely slow down our mutual helpfulness for life's journey. Anytime we feel defensive or want somebody off our back, all we need to say is "I feel like you're judging me," and the person is gone in a flash.

But like mountain climbers, we are supposed to be helping to pull each other up the mountain. We have given up a great deal of that help by excessive application of certain slogans: *I can't save anyone but myself. I know I can't rescue him. She's got to find the truth for herself. Who am I to judge? Live and let live. Do your own thing.*

There is certainly a kernel of truth in them all, in the sense of allowing others primary responsibility for their own climb. But that does not mean we leave each other completely alone on the cliffs. We all need a rope tossed to us every now and then, or instructions shouted from above when a friend sees us inching toward hazardous ground. Even when we feel our friends are mistaken, we can thank them for caring instead of turning on them and calling them judgmental.

This judgment hysteria could lead us into a very lonely age, in which people are packed in with each other like sardines yet increasingly afraid to touch or be touched very deeply. I think many people already feel this way. The popular concept of "support"—another buzzword—means apparently only to encourage, not to instruct or change. This leaves us dreadfully on our own in a way that makes it much more difficult to find our way up the sacred mountain.

At a prison conference in Chicago a few years ago, one of the speakers described his well-known mentoring program for ex-cons. It sounded like a wonderful project, but I was jolted by the vehemence in his voice when he said, "And I'll tell you one thing that mentoring does *not* mean: telling someone else what to do!" The audience applauded wildly and some people even cheered. The speaker and conference-goers were obviously celebrating and reaffirming a popular idea together.

I sat there scratching my head in wonder. First, the statement itself is not completely honest; it's playing with words. Anyone who works with dysfunctional or marginally functional people hopes to tell them some basic important things to do and not to do. Do we force our children to learn to ride a bike without giving them a few dos and don'ts to minimize injuries?

Second, there's nothing wrong in telling people what to do sometimes. It is not necessarily judgmental, and it's as crucial as knowing when *not* to tell them what to do. Let's not become so philosophically simplistic that we can't handle more than one side of a coin. The truth is, sometimes the right thing is to tell others what to do, and sometimes the right thing is to let them figure it out for themselves. We can be judgmental or nonjudgmental either way.

I know a very dear woman who counsels prisoners. She is exceptionally motivated and compassionate. She sees her role as being a "sacred, safe space for someone to open up and be whoever they are without my judging or trying to change them in any way." Child molesters and murderers can sit with her and go into elaborate details about sexual or violent fantasies they may have, and she will simply listen with an open heart and accept them as they are.

For the life of me, I have not come across any sacred scripture advising us to merely listen and not discern right from wrong—maybe a misguided pocket of pop psychology, but not a wisdom tradition. The great teachings are clear: there is the Great Undivided Perfection, but within perfection there is a right path and wrong path—dharma and adharma in the East, good and evil in the West—and we are instructed to absolutely take a stand to try to save our brothers or sisters from destroying their spiritual lives by doing wrong. Is it judgmental to say that it is wrong to fantasize about molesting a child? We should remember that when Cain responded to God's query about Abel by saying, "I am not my brother's keeper," it was not the answer God wanted!

It's not that hard to understand what judging really means: We must not feel superior to anyone. We must never look down our noses at anyone, or assume that we are incapable of committing the same vices and sins as others. Being nonjudgmental does not mean we are to become "value neutral" regarding morality, ethics, virtue, and vice.

But isn't this a large part of our problem about judging or not judging? Have we slipped into a modern value-neutral philosophy that says right and wrong are always relative, and are up to each of us to decide for ourselves? Is this why we allow ourselves and our children to watch movies (with unbelievably real special effects) in which human beings get brutally beaten or raped, or shot to death, or hacked up with chainsaws and axes? This may be a sincere and profound philosophical confusion we need to look at so that we can take more appropriate control over our lives and our childrens' lives.

It's easy to see one source of this confusion. The past thirty years of Western culture have seen a dangerous slide regarding what is popularly called our shadow side. In the 1960s, many of us recognized that we were living in denial of this shadow self, or dark part of our nature. Such denial leads to hypocrisy and sanctimoniousness, so we began to say, "Let's acknowledge our shadow" as an expression of newfound maturity and humility. Of course, all the wisdom traditions have always said the same thing: all potential for good and evil resides within each of us.

But along the way, for reasons involving intersections between psychology, consumerism, and the entertainment industry, we went from "Acknowledge your shadow," to "Make friends with your shadow," to "Celebrate your shadow." An anxious idea began to creep into our minds that it was actually unhealthy not to delve into our lusts, our rage, our darkest fantasies, our greed—all the shadow qualities of human nature that every ancient tradition has encouraged us to keep in check.

The Greek wisdom tradition called the shadow Pandora's box. Once we open it up, it is nearly impossible to put the lid back on; especially in modern times, when we may mistakenly believe it is unhealthy to put the lid back on. The lowest, basest facets of our human nature have come to be seen as natural drives that must be given their due. Self-control, the cornerstone of every path to enlightenment, is seen as repression. Indulging the shadow side has become a prime target of moviemaking, the music industry, and consumer marketing. We need to refresh our biggest view of this whole mess about right and wrong and judging.

The basic values of dharma and adharma, of good and evil, do not change from age to age. They are not meant to be reinvented in each era, either individually or democratically. They are meant to be passed on, instilled, and strengthened in each of us with help from others.

In fact, the Sanskrit word *dharma* actually comes from root syllables meaning "to hold back from disaster." The Ten Commandments, Buddhist precepts, Hindu Yamas and Niyamas, Islamic codes—all these have been handed down to hold us back from the very sort of moral and psychological disasters that abound in our age. We have plenty of timeless wisdom to draw on. We just need to think and act independently of the prevailing moods of modern culture.

In a sense, the spiritual path is almost nothing more than constant discernment between right and wrong, good and bad, skillful and unskillful. We discern for ourselves, and we often share discernment with others. We certainly can't wait until we're enlightened before we do this. We would never get enlightened that way.

At some point we have to begin calling things as we see them, in a spirit of goodwill and good humor, realizing that of course we'll turn out to be mistaken sometimes, but that's okay so long as we don't pretend to be infallible. As long as this period of "judgment hysteria" continues, we will not be fully engaged with each other, not fully taking the roller-coaster ride of life, able to argue or agree, support or not support, every now and then to lay into each other out of love and concern.

I deeply appreciate the people in my life who have told me things I did not want to hear at the time. How impoverished we are without our friends' frank and blunt opinions! What are we so afraid of? We can take it. Influencing each other for the best is an important expression of a caring community.

A Practice: TALKING CIRCLE—DISCERNING VERSUS JUDGING

This practice is very simple to explain, because it will create itself once you get it going. Gather at least one or two friends (or spouse, family, co-workers) for an open discussion of this very topic. Bring up some simple questions to kick off a discussion, such as the following:

- What are some examples of judging and discernment in our circle?
- Do I use the fear of being called judgmental as an excuse to avoid confrontations?
- What does supportiveness mean to me? Is it solely positive?
- In how many ways would my friends be surprised to know how I honestly feel about their behavior and path?
- What is my reaction when I am accused of being judgmental? Do I shut down?
- What does it mean to be a truly supportive friend? What happens when I think my friend is wrong?
- Are we benefiting from each other's friendship as much as we could?
- Could we all agree, as a circle of friends, to loosen the leash a little and feel freer to influence each other without having our heads bitten off for trying?
- Can we agree to a temporary moratorium on the phrase "Stop being judgmental"?

Perhaps one of your friends occasionally mentions that she and her husband use pornography to enhance their sex life.

Let's say you feel, as I do, that porn magazines and videos are part of a harmful industry that exploits and demeans many young people, and contributes to the links between sex and violence, sex and money, and sex and infidelity. Let's say you feel it is wrong to support such an industry by your patronage.

You have several options in situations like this. You can conceal your true feelings in order to appear nonjudgmental. But then you run the risk of being a false friend, pretending to go along with something that actually offends you. You can demand that she and her husband stop using pornography if they wish to remain your friends. But that becomes a power play over the importance of your friendship, which skirts the main issue. Or you can let your friend know that you love her and want to remain her friend, but that you hope she and her husband will reconsider their involvement in pornography, and then honestly explain why you feel the way you do. If they do not wish to reconsider how they feel, then at least they can cease to discuss that part of their life with you, so you need not be put in awkward positions time and time again.

This is the tack many of my white Southern friends took with their families in the heyday of civil rights. They tried lovingly to convince their families to feel differently about black people, and then said at least to please not make racial jokes or slurs in their presence. They did not usually find it necessary to abandon their families altogether, but did feel the need to bring their relationship into truth. And for the most part, it deepened their relationships and influenced all the parties to some degree. It is good to influence each other properly; let's not forget that.

Every Mother's Child

I understand service to others is based on compassion and kindness even toward those who've done awful things. How can I feel kind toward those who have committed terrible deeds or who live with completely different values than my own?

We must try to understand that kindness, compassion, forgiveness, and genuine goodwill are the basic tenets of every wisdom tradition. They are not new ideas, and are not merely suggestions or naïve notions. They are instructions from above. If we follow the instructions, we will thrive; if not, we will suffer. It's not a philosophy, it's a fact. This is the most important thing to consider when we struggle with our feelings of hatred, revenge, or indifference. Our backs are against the wall; we cannot have fully meaningful lives until we come to terms with these universal teachings of compassion. It may be a long process of development, but you will have taken a huge step forward when you surrender to the irrefutability of this.

According to the wisdom traditions, hatred, vengeance, ill will, or even cold disregard are never life-affirming responses. Such malignant feelings may tempt us mightily when we are the victim of a crime or a personal betrayal, but then we're supposed to struggle with our consciences, wrestle with the moral/ethical/spiritual values we embrace, and try to put things back into a perspective that humanizes us once again. This has been a natural process since the beginning of time. It's a big part of the way we learn and grow.

To me, one of the most frightening social developments of the twentieth century is the way we have permitted ourselves to come out into the open with an enormous amount of anger, mean-spiritedness, and vengeance toward criminals and other populations we don't like. All the stops have been pulled, and our politicians express this modern virulence without even a pretense of belief in the human spirit's ability to repent and change.

The spiritual powers of the universe will not judge us by the crimes that have been committed against us. They will judge us by how we respond. These days, we are responding with socially sanctioned hatred and brutality, with execution parties outside prisons, with inhuman, futuristic "supermax" prisons that drive people crazy rather than encourage them to change for the better.

If we wish to be in tune with the best human values, we must change our attitudes toward those who wrong us. That doesn't mean we allow people to hurt us or rob us or harm our communities. It doesn't mean we become pushovers or idiots. After all, we don't allow our children to exploit us or do cruel or immoral things as they are growing up, but when they do, we don't hate them for it. We don't punish them so viciously that they can hardly function for the rest of their lives. We don't throw them out of our hearts and tell them to fend for themselves forever.

Every prisoner is some mother's child, and we *do* throw prisoners out of our hearts forever in our present criminal justice system. By venting our rage and hatred, we make everything worse. We make people worse. We take many confused, mostly selfish, young men and women who could easily be turned around by kindness and skills training, and instead we traumatize them so much that we create a criminal underclass of dysfunctional, alienated people who can never find their way back into decent society. No words could possibly exaggerate the magnitude of the spiritual mistake we have been making in our criminal justice system. We are hurting ourselves unimaginably, and the consequences will be felt for many generations to come. I pray we come to our senses soon.

We are also forgetting that many of the greatest saints and sages of all religions were once criminals, drunkards, prostitutes, and even killers. Saint Paul was once Saul of Tarsus, a vicious bigot and killer of Christians. The great Tibetan saint Milarepa was once a vile sorcerer who murdered thirty-seven people. Valmiki, one of the foremost sages of Hinduism, was once a drunkard, a thief, and a killer. These saints were truly terrible, cruel people early in their lives, far more evil than millions of the hapless souls we lock up in prisons nowadays.

Religious history is filled with such redeemed, transformed sages. If we give up our belief in redemption and transformation, we are crossing a very serious line, which will render us poor indeed. Some potential sages and humanitarians of our times are languishing in prison cells right now. I have had the good fortune to meet many of them. Redemption and transformation are the most wonderful parts of any religious faith. Are we sure we want to abandon those parts of the creed? This is not "us against them." This is "us against the highest principles of human conduct." Which means, ultimately, this is "us against us." Please try to see what is at stake here.

• • •

Another problem with unkindness and ill will toward criminals is that those qualities spread like infections into all areas of our personal and national life. Is it any surprise that there is no dignity or decorum left in the way our political leaders speak to or about each other? Is it any surprise that trash talk shows on television feature pathetic people who scream at and lunge violently for each other while the audience hoots and hollers? We have experienced a serious decline of even the most basic sense of courtesy.

I pulled into a gas station recently to ask directions. Two women, both thirtyish, well-dressed, nice-looking, were standing by their cars pumping gas. I addressed both of them, because they were only about three feet apart, and asked how to find a local builder's supply. One woman said, "If you continue down this road about another mile, you'll come to an intersection . . ." She paused a second to think, and the other woman cheerfully interjected, "It's a real big intersection." The first woman glared at her and snapped, "I was speaking, thank you! I don't need your help to give him directions!"

The second woman turned away in embarrassment, and the woman who had yelled finished giving me the directions in a pleasant tone, as though nothing had happened. These were two strangers who didn't have a thing against each other a moment earlier. As I drove away, their bodies were still only three feet away from each other, but their hearts were a thousand miles apart. How sad for us all. This unfortunate incident took place not on any mean streets, but in a small town in North Carolina, where generations of citizens have prided themselves on friendliness and Southern hospitality.

I'm worried that for many of us, our predominant attitude has become testy self-assertion rather than cooperativeness or even courtesy. And why not? That's practically all we see when we turn on the television or pick up a magazine or attend a town meeting about whether to buy a new school bus or put a cross atop city hall during the Christmas holidays. Everyone seems so willing to be rude and angry over anything at all! Are we becoming so aggressive that the meanest and nastiest among us can rise to the top of the power structure because we have more faith in those qualities than we do in goodness and diplomacy? We'd better be careful.

The hatred and rage we express toward criminals is not a separate issue from these other problems. We are breaking a fundamental spiritual law, and the price we are paying for it is increased rudeness, mean-spiritedness, crime, violence, depravity, and of course more hatred and rage. To put it bluntly, we are turning against each other, often even in our own families. "Tough love" toward recalcitrant adolescents is sometimes necessary, but many people misunderstand and misuse tough love in order to express anger and bitterness toward their own children. Again, we'd better be careful. We are treading on very thin ice here.

I can recall a wonderful example of the opposite behavior, of unshakable goodwill. In 1994, at a small college in North Carolina, His Holiness the Dalai Lama was hosted by Senator Jesse Helms, who is known as one of the world's most stubborn arch-conservatives. One of our board members who attended the event said she was astonished and deeply moved by Senator Helms's affectionate, respectful introduction of the Dalai Lama. Helms addressed him as "Your Holiness"; he kissed him, they bowed to each other in humility. A cynic might say the only thing they like about each other is their mutual political opposition to China, but many people who were there insisted that their goodwill felt both mutual and sincere.

My guru once said, "When a pickpocket looks at a saint, all he can see are his pockets." From my experiences with holy men and holy women, I am sure that the converse holds true as well: when a saint looks at a pickpocket, all he can see is a latent saint. Could it be that when most of us look at Jesse Helms we see his pockets, and when the Dalai Lama looks he sees the saint that's lurking deep down inside? And could it be that Jesse Helms may feel the Dalai Lama's respect and goodwill, and he then rises to the occasion, responding in a way that may even surprise himself?

Matthew, the heartless tax collector, went to Peter's home to mock Jesus. Jesus welcomed him, invited him to dinner. Peter was outraged at that, so Jesus told Matthew he would come to his home for dinner—totally unthinkable for a respectable person to do. Matthew, too, rose to the occasion. Before long he became a disciple—and eventually the saint Jesus could see from the moment they met.

A few years ago I gave a talk at a law school in Winston-Salem, North Carolina. When it came time for questions from the audience, a big fellow in his thirties stood up in the back, very nervous, and told a fascinating story. He said, "I don't have a question. I just want to say thanks to Bo and Sita Lozoff for something they don't even know about. I spent most of my life in juvenile halls and prisons until just a few years ago. I want to tell you, my whole life was based around accepting that I was a bad seed, a rotten apple. I accepted it, I was comfortable with it. I had no plans to change it. One time, Bo and Sita came in to do a talk or something, and they just happened to look me right in the eyes. I gave them every ounce of badness I could, but they just kept looking at me like I was a good person.

"Well, I tell you," he continued, "that done freaked me out. I mean it, I hated their guts for that. They tore my life apart with one look. I hated them, I really did. I could never again convince myself that I was rotten. And if I wasn't rotten, then I knew I had to change. Now I'm a student in this university and I just want to say thank you, Bo and Sita, for seeing something in me that I didn't even know about."

A Practice: RADICAL GOODWILL

This is fitting for the last practice of this book, because it is the ultimate practice of unilateral, no-excuses Community with everyone, everywhere. It started merely as a daily blessing to my son, Josh. At the end of my morning meditation practice, I used to bring him into my heart for a moment, feel all my fatherly affection, and offer him a blessing for the day. Soon I began to understand that the feeling I call fatherly affection is much the same as the radical goodwill that the Dalai Lama feels for Jesse Helms: it's an absolute acceptance of his decency, his goodness.

I know my son is a good person. No matter what mistakes he might make, I know his true nature is good. I probably know it better than he does—just like Jesus toward Matthew. Regardless of sins, addictions, insanity, crimes, there would be no way to convince me my son is a bad person. Radical Goodwill is to know the same thing about everyone on earth—obviously not an easy task, but possible with practice.

The ironic thing is, this practice will do more for you than for all those you bless. To rid our hearts of ill will, resentment, grudges, bitterness, anger is an unbelievable blessing, truly heaven here on earth. Whenever we may think along the lines of whether someone "deserves" our forgiveness, we are already missing the point of radical goodwill. Forgiveness and blessings are essential for our perfection, not just for the people we forgive and bless.

- Begin this practice by bringing into your mind and heart whomever you love most sweetly in the whole world, preferably an innocent, such as a baby or even a cherished pet. Let your heart glow and smile as you feel your love for this being. Bless him or her.
- Then strengthen your awareness of the soft, open feeling in your heart, and begin bringing the image of other people into that very place, seeing them as sweetly as the one you started with, and offering them a blessing with no strings attached.
- As you feel your heart close, bring back the image of your original loved one to open it once again, and then continue. This way, the love you have for that one special being will truly help you in a very practical way to deepen your love for all of God's children.
- Gradually, as this practice becomes more comfortable, you will want to bring to mind all the difficult, ornery, or lost people you can imagine (no problem finding enough of them!) and strengthen your belief in their goodness, their decency, trying to know it as well as you know it about the most innocent being you started with.

Besides people in your personal life, you can apply this practice to the latest objects of modern scorn and hatred—the juveniles who kill their classmates, a terrorist who blows up an airplane, a serial killer, a child molester, any other human being the media holds up as a monster for the nation to hate. If you and I consider ourselves spiritual pilgrims, we cannot join in with such mob mentalities. Like St. Francis's prayer, wherever there is hatred, we must sow love. We have no choice. This practice is a powerful tool for actually doing it, rather than merely believing in it.

Think of this practice as learning to see every human being as though his or her mother were your next-door neighbor. If you take the time to practice this every day even for a few seconds, you will gradually come to see that there is no one you don't know. It might even begin to sink in that you yourself, down deep, are a saint or angel as well. So you may as well start acting like it.

> Give to the one who asks you,
> And do not turn away from the one
> who wants to borrow from you.
> Love your enemies,
> and pray for those who persecute you,
> For if you love only those who love you,
> What reward shall you have?
> And if you greet only your brothers,
> what are you doing more than others?
> Do not even sinners do the same?
> Be perfect, as your Father in heaven is perfect.
> —Jesus, the Sermon on the Mount

Afterword:
Keeping It Simple

In the mid-1960s, Sita and I struck up a lifelong friendship with a three-hundred-pound hillbilly truckdriver named Ted. Ted had become an instant celebrity in the civil rights movement after knocking out a sheriff's deputy who was about to brutalize a black co-worker of Ted's. Ted didn't see himself as any sort of activist—he could barely read and write. He merely responded to a bad situation as a genuine human being.

Ted had already spent nine years in prison in Nebraska, where he was born, and then migrated to Florida with his wife and four kids to start a new life. Living in dire poverty, he and his family were good, decent folks with tremendous capability and common sense. Sita and I stayed with them off and on, and Ted's wife, Elsie, taught Sita a lot about farm cooking and canning and all sorts of things that proved invaluable later on. Sita and I drifted away and went through profound changes, getting into meditation and yoga and Eastern spiritual views. Several years passed before

Ted and Elsie came to visit us at the ashram we were living in. We were wearing white clothes and long prayer beads. We had become vegetarians and were oh-so-gentle. Ted asked us to explain what the hell we were doing.

I responded with eloquent, long-winded truths about spirituality and illusion and meditation and transformation and the chakras and breathing and energy and . . . you get the point. Ted looked straight into my eyes the whole time. When I finished, he spit out a little chewing tobacco and said something that has shaped my work, my writing, and my speaking, ever since: "You know, Bo, if you can't say all this stuff simple enough for me to understand, then that means one of two things: either what you're saying is bull-shit, or else you don't understand it yourself."

That was one of the truest and deepest lessons anyone has ever taught me. Ted has long since, as they would say in Tibet, "departed for more fortunate rebirths," but his un-pretentious wisdom lives on in this book and in the way I hope you will integrate the practices into your life. If we don't keep it reasonably simple, we will miss the point again and again.

Your lifestyle may change. The spiritual practices you choose may change. But always, spiritual practice should help you become more caring, not less; more resilient and good-humored and adaptable, not less. When you feel you've painted yourself into a corner and are at odds with your whole environment, then it's time to step back and take a simpler look once again. Love people and love your own life. Take it easy on God's creation and help out when-ever you can.

When a rope is knotted up in complicated ways, it may take a lot of effort and various skills to untie all the knots and have a smooth rope. The many practices in this book are just various ways of unknotting the rope. You may begin with simple breathing or meditation, then add prayer, maybe do daily sacred readings. Be careful not to tie even more knots in your rope with your spiritual practices. As dear old Ted reminded me, keep it simple.

One practical way to keep it simple is to consciously choose a practice and think about what time of day you can realistically make it part of your schedule. Try to consider in advance what you might need to start. Do you need a quiet space to meditate? Is there a place in your home that will work? Do you have a pillow to sit on so you can be comfortable? Do you have whatever books you want to read from? If your practice involves writing, do you have pen and paper? These might seem like obvious questions, but gathering whatever you need ahead of time will help you avoid unnecessary knots in the rope.

It may seem complicated to practice more service, or to sustain such practice. You can always start on a very small (yet infinitely valuable) scale by practicing simple loving-kindness with everyone you encounter, from grocery clerks to toll booth collectors. One kind step naturally leads to another.

When we integrate committed service into our lifestyle, the temptation may arise to lighten up on the time spent in personal spiritual practices. But I believe that's what leads to burnout for so many people. Trying to dedicate yourself entirely through outward activity, no matter how much you seem to be helping others, will sooner or later chew you up and spit you out if you don't take time for inner silence as well. It's like trying to breathe out all the time without breathing in. How long can that last? Be sure you breathe in, too, so that you're helping others from a deeper place.

> A guy goes to his spiritual master and says, "My problem is, I've been trying to faithfully devote an hour a day to meditation, but I have a wife and three kids, a demanding job; the kids are up when I awake, and there's so much going on when I get home, and my wife and I need to spend time together at night. Tell me what I should do." The master replies, "*Two* hours a day."

As the inner work of Communion strengthens our presence, clears our minds and opens our hearts, the outer work of Community becomes a natural, unforced manifestation of that presence, clarity and compassion. This is the only way I know to have a truly full-bodied life, with head and heart in a spontaneous, ever-shifting balance.

No matter how good-natured or well-intentioned we are, it doesn't seem possible to live a life of joyful service without learning an inner-outer rhythm. Service, maybe, but not joyful service. That's the advanced course, and it requires jumping into the pot as an ingredient, rather than neatly stirring from above.

At Kindness House, we have weekly tunings, or house meetings, to check in with ourselves and with each other. These are essentially talking circles, where we can focus on our friendship and spiritual work without phones ringing, visitors coming up the driveway, or any other distractions. You can do the same thing, alone or with friends, by considering some basic questions from time to time:

- Do I believe in the life I am living?
- Do I allot enough of my time to spiritual practice? To service?
- Am I taking proper care of my body? Getting enough sleep and exercise?
- Am I replacing bad habits with better ones?
- Do I spend more money than I need to? Why?
- Do I enjoy my livelihood?
- How did I treat each person I encountered today?
- Do the significant people in my life know how much I appreciate them?

However you phrase such "spiritual reality-check" questions to yourself and your family or friends, keep them simple. These are the fundamental elements of your life—your values, how you spend your time, how you take care of yourself, how you treat others. It is not only sensible to ask these questions, it is crucial to a meaningful life. It may feel awkward at first, but so did riding a bike or even learning how to walk. It just takes practice.

s, Sages, and Sacred Texts
Mentioned in This Book

The ADI GRANTH are the scriptures of Sikhism, and contain around six thousand hymns. The Hindu and Muslim influences are apparent, evidence of the origins of Sikhism.

BA'AL SHEM Tov is the popular name of Rabbi Yisrael Ben Eliezer (1700–1760), founder of the Hasidic movement in Judaism. *Ba'al Shem Tov* is translated in several ways, including "Master of the Name." Miracles abounded around the Ba'al Shem Tov, and it is said that when he prayed, bright light emanated from him and even the room he stood in sometimes shook.

The BHAGAVAD GITA, Sanskrit for "The Song of the Lord," is a section of the Mahabharata, one of Hinduism's two great sacred epics, the other being the Ramayana (see below). The Bhavagad Gita's main message is the abandonment of ego in service to God. The Gita was Mahatma Gandhi's primary spiritual scripture, which he read daily.

BAHA' U'LLAH (1817–1892) was a Persian religious leader who founded an offshoot of Islam called Bahaism. He spent much of his life in prison, and wrote the major Baha'i text, Kitabi Ikan or "The Book of Certitude."

BUDDHA was born as Siddhartha Gautama (ca. 563–480 B.C.), a wealthy prince. Many miracles occurred around his birth, and the sages told his father, the king, that Siddhartha was destined either to be a great king or a great saint. His father became determined to make sure it was the former, not the latter, so he sheltered his child from seeing any suffering, old age, disease, or death. Eventually Siddhartha came in contact with a sick person, an old person, a funeral procession, and a sage. The transient nature of worldly life ruined his enjoyment of royal pleasures, and he renounced everything in search of a deeper truth. He achieved *nirvana,* the state beyond suffering, while meditating under a Bodhi tree. He then spent the rest of his life as the *Buddha,* or "awakened one," teaching many disciples the simple "middle way" to discover one's true nature and the nature of all existence.

RABBI SHLOMO CARLEBACH (1924–1994) was rabbi of Kihillat Jacob in Manhattan and American Judaism's most popular Hasidic songwriter/folksinger.

His Holiness the fourteenth DALAI LAMA is the political and religious leader of the Tibetan people. Since his exile to India following the Chinese occupation of Tibet in 1959, the Dalai Lama has become known as one of the world's most beloved humanitarians and spiritual leaders by people of all faiths. Tibetan Buddhists consider the Dalai Lama to be a reincarnation of Avalokitesvara, the Buddha of Compassion.

TULSI DAS (1532–1623) was India's premier folk-poet. He rewrote the Ramayana, one of India's two great sacred epics, from Sanskrit into Hindi to make the sublime story accessible to common people. Tulsi Das's version, the Ramacharitamanas, has become the most popular sacred story of India, performed and read, sung and told in every medium.

THE DHAMMAPADA, meaning "The Path of Virtue" in Pali, is a primary Buddhist scripture that describes the main values of life and the Buddha's way to enlightenment.

SAINT FRANCIS OF ASSISI (ca. 1181–1226) was an important figure in the medieval church. He gave up an affluent, privileged life to devote himself to Christ's teachings of poverty, simplicity, and love for all. Francis founded his own order of monks by 1210.

MAHATMA GANDHI (1869–1948) devoted his life to the Hindu idea of *ahimsa,* or nonviolence. His successful campaign to free India from British rule brought Gandhi worldwide admiration and respect. Gandhi's personal courage and penetrating analyses of social change have been a primary influence on non-violent political movements worldwide, including Martin Luther King's civil rights struggle in the United States. Gandhi was assassinated in 1947 by a Sikh zealot. His last words were *"Jai Ram"* ("Hail God" in Hindi).

KAHLIL GIBRAN (1883–1931), who was born in Lebanon and later lived in New York, was a poet and novelist. Gibran is most known for *The Prophet* and *Jesus, the Son of Man.* Both works are a fusion of Eastern and Western poetic mysticism.

The CHRISTIAN GOSPELS from the core of the New Testament in the Bible. They narrate the life and teachings of Jesus from the viewpoints of evangelists Matthew, Mark, Luke, and John.

HAFIZ (1320–1389) is one of Islam's most treasured mystical poets. Mad with love for God, outrageous in his humor and metaphors, brilliant translations of Hafiz's poetry by Daniel Ladinsky can be found in the books *I Heard God Laughing, The Gift,* and *The Subject Tonight Is Love.*

HILLEL was a Jewish rabbi and teacher living in the first century B.C. in Jerusalem. He used examples and pithy sayings to interpret the Scriptures and helped shape Jewish thought.

The JATAKA TALES is a collection of 547 stories of Buddha in his past lives. In each story, Buddha is disguised as something other than himself (usually an animal), and each story works to illustrate a specific moral.

JESUS OF NAZARETH (ca. 6 B.C.–A.D. 33) is considered by Christians to be the Christ, the savior of the world, the son of God. Jesus arose from the Jewish tradition at the time of Rome's oppression of the Jewish people. He was crucified for his and his followers' assertion that he was indeed the Messiah promised by God throughout the Old Testament. The majority of Jesus' direct teachings are recounted in the Sermon on the Mount, and focus on direct, radical abandonment of all selfish and self-protective behavior in order to devote ourselves to the service of God through service to all his creatures. Countless miracles occurred around him, including his own resurrection from the dead, which is celebrated by Christians as Easter.

FATHER MATTHEW KELTY is a monk of Gethsemane and former novice of Thomas Merton's, who spent nine years living as a religious solitary in New Guinea. His book, *My Song Is of Mercy,* is both Christian and universally spiritual.

The KORAN is Islam's sacred scripture and means in Arabic "the reading" or "the lesson." In seventh-century Persia, Muhammad (see below) heard a voice telling him to write down the revelations of God and to become His messenger. Muslims consider that voice to have been the archangel Gabriel. Reluctant at first, Muhammad became the Prophet, or the Messenger, and founder of Islam. The Islamic faith is a branch of the Judeo-Christian tree, and embraces Old and New Testament figures as prophets of God, including Jesus. Many Muslims consider it a sacred duty to memorize the entire 75,000-word Koran in its original Persian language exactly as revealed by the Prophet.

KRISHNA is considered by Hindus to be a human embodiment of the supreme Lord, Vishnu. Like Jesus, he was born in very humble surroundings (in Kirshna's case, a dungeon) and was the object of a massive search by an evil king to destroy him as an infant (as was Jesus by Herod). Krishna and his brother, Balaram, were given to humble cowherds to raise in anonymity. Many miracles attended his life, and he revealed his identity fully at age twelve (also similar to Jesus' first preaching in the temple at Jerusalem). Krishna is the pivotal figure in the Mahabharata, and his central teachings comprise the Bhagavad Gita.

JIDDU KRISHNAMURTI (1895–1986). An Indian spiritual teacher who focused on self-awareness in contrast to outside authority such as religion or gurus, he was born in India and later settled in Ojai, California, where the Krishnamurti Foundation continues today. His books include *Commentaries on Living, Freedom from the Unknown, The First and Last Freedom, Life in Freedom,* and *Think on These Things.*

LAO-TZU (sixth century B.C.), a Chinese historian and scholar is considered the founder of Taoism. He wrote the Tao Te Ching, which translates as "Classic of the Way and its Virtue." His oral teachings are expressed in the Hua Hu Ching. Taoism emphasizes simplicity and attunement to the nature of all things, and is similar to Buddhism in its focus on moving beyond the sense of self, as exemplified in the quintessential Taoist expression, "The sage does nothing, and nothing remains undone."

MAHABHARATA is one of the two great sacred stories of the Hindu faith. It was known as far back as the sixth century B.C., and is attributed to the sage Vyasa. Through the story of a powerful family dynasty and its internal quarrels among cousins vying for rulership of India, the Mahabharata provides intricate insights and teachings into self-mastery and devotion to God. Its section called the Bhagavad Gita has long been considered by people of many faiths to be among the world's most profound scriptures. An excellent modern version of Mahabharata, minus the Gita, was translated by William Buck and is published by the University of California Press.

MILAREPA (1040–1123) was a Buddhist yogi, saint, and poet who earlier in his life had been a sorcerer responsible for the deaths of many people. He is one of the central figures in the Kagyu lineage of Tibetan Buddhism.

FATHER MIGUEL MOLINOS (1628–1696) was a favorite priest in the Vatican when he wrote about a devotional, mystical aspect of Catholicism and published *The Spiritual Guide* in 1675. Convicted of heresy and sentenced to life imprisonment for his beliefs, Molinos died in the Vatican dungeon. The Pope issued a decree that anyone found in possession of his book would be excommunicated. That decree has never been retracted.

MOTHER TERESA (1910–1997) was born in Albania, but lived and worked in Calcutta, India, devoting her life to serving the most destitute in society. Her Sisters of Charity missions are now spread around the world, and Mother Teresa's name itself has become the modern standard for selfless service. In her own view, she served God, not man. Her life centered around prayer, and she once confided, "When I look into the eyes of a dying beggar, I see the Christ." She emphasized an attitude of genuine gladness of heart when serving the poor, not pity.

MUHAMMAD (570–632) was a middle-aged man when he first started having visions. When he moved north of Mecca in 622 to be closer to supporters, the start of Islam was born. Years later, in a bloodless siege, he reclaimed the city of Mecca yet chose to live in Medina. Influenced by Judaism and Christianity, he preached monotheism as the central idea of Islam. He is considered by Muslims to be the chosen messenger of God.

MURSHID SAMUEL "Sufi Sam" LEWIS (1896–1971) was a forerunner of universal religion and unitive mystical experience in our time. He embraced and taught Sufism as well as Zen Buddhism and other spiritual paths. His writings include *Spiritual Dance and Walk, Talks of an American Sufi,* and *This Is the New Age in Person.*

NEEM KAROLI BABA, my own guru, was a mysterious Indian saint who began appearing in my dreams when I was around eight years old. I called him my "Magic Man," and had no idea he really existed until seeing a photo of him in Ram Dass's first book, *Be Here Now.* He was said to be somewhere between eighty and three hundred years old when he left his body in 1973. Remaining nearly unknown, he is directly responsible for the Prison-Ashram Project and some of the most enduring good works of our age, including the eradication of smallpox. Miracles abounded in his presence. Books about him include *Miracle of Love, By His Grace,* and *The Near and the Dear.*

The NEW TESTAMENT is the Christian portion of the Bible, and consists of the Gospels, Acts of the Apostles, Epistles, and Revelations. The Gospels, by Matthew, Mark, Luke, and John, recount the story of Jesus' life. The Acts of the Apostles relay the teachings of Peter and Paul, two important followers of Jesus. The Epistles are letters. Revelations deals with predictions of the future and the Last Judgment.

The OLD TESTAMENT comprises the Jewish scriptures in the Bible, and consists of the Torah, the Prophets, and the Writings. The Torah's five books, Genesis, Exodus, Leviticus, Numbers, and Deuteronomy, recount the Jewish story of creation and declare laws. The books of the Prophets focus on the teachings of the Jewish prophets. Writings is a melange of many different things including psalms, accounts of history, proverbs, and stories.

SAINT PAUL (ca. 3–67), originally Saul of Tarsus, was an enemy of Christianity who, like the Tibetan saint Milarepa (see above), was responsible for many deaths before his conversion. Through his letters to early congregations, he wrote most of the

New Testament—often from Roman prison cells, where he spent much of his later life.

RAMAKRISHNA (1836–1886) was a Bengali saint and mystic who directly experienced God through the images of all the major religions. Ramakrishna taught that every religion is a different path to the same experience of God. His disciples, including Swami Vivekananda, have had a tremendous impact on the world's interfaith dialogue. The best-known book of Ramakriskna's teachings is *The Gospel of Ramakrishna.*

RAMAYANA is one of the two great ancient epics of Hinduism, and the core book of my own family's spiritual practice. The story involves God's descent to earth as Rama, or Ram, and his wife, Sita. It is a story of adventure and intrigue and devotion and honor. It is the story of your life and my life, and how to emerge victorious from our inevitable struggles. An excellent modern version of Ramayana was translated by William Buck and is published by the University of California Press.

FATHER MURRAY ROGERS is a priest of the Church of England, and a personal mentor to my family and community. Father Murray and his wife, Mary, along with their committed friend Heather Sandeman, spent twenty-seven years in India living among the poor, then ten years in monastic community in Israel, ten years in China, and several years in Canada before returning to their native England. They have practiced truly simple living and spiritual activism for longer than I have been alive, and are radiantly humble, joyful elders who inspire us and keep us on our toes.

JALĀL AL-DĪN-AR-RŪMĪ (1207–1273) is the best-known Persian mystical poet. Rumi lived in what is now called Turkey. He wrote *Mathnawi,* a six-volume work of spiritual teaching and Sufi lore. *Mathnawi* has been a great influence, known or memorized by most of the Persian speaking world.

RABBI RAMI SHAPIRO is a personal friend and one of the most creative voices in contemporary American Judaism. His books include *Open Secrets, Minyan,* and *Wisdom of the Jewish Sages.*

The SIKH religion evolved out of a union of Islam and Hinduism. It was begun by Kabir, a Muslim. It espouses equality of all men despite caste, iconoclasm, and brotherly love. Nanak (d. 1539) was the first of the ten principle gurus of the Sikh religion.

SUFISM, a mystical sect of Islam, shares with Hasidic Judaism a focus on intense fervor and longing for God and ecstatic dancing and singing. Sufism has produced some of the finest spiritual poetry of all time.

A SWAMI is a Hindu spiritual teacher and ascetic who lives a disciplined life of service and religious devotion.

TAO TE CHING, by Lao-Tzu, is one of the world's great spiritual classics. Brief, philosophical, and mystically enigmatic, it focuses on the virtue of Tao, "the natural way," the eternal universal principle.

FATHER THEOPHANE is another personal friend and elder whose book *Tales of a Magic Monastery* is a priceless collection of very short stories—some only a paragraph or two—expressing the mystery, peace, wit and devotion of a lifelong follower of Jesus' way. Father Theophane lives at St. Benedict's Monastery in Snowmass, Colorado.

THERESA OF AVILA (1515–1582), the first woman ever honored by the Pope, lived in Spain and wrote a spiritual autobiography with a treatise on prayer called *Life. Relations, Way of Perfection,* and *Interior Castle* are her other works. She is widely regarded as one of the most passionate devotional voices in the Christian tradition.

The UPANISHADS, the last sections of the Hindu Vedic scriptures, deal with the great mysteries of all life and existence. They are among the world's greatest timeless scriptures.

VALMIKI (ca. 6000 B.C.) is known in India as the "Adi-Kavya," or "First Poet." Like Milarepa and Saint Paul and many other saints, Valmiki was a criminal, a killer who was transformed after a chance meeting with a sage. He then spent so many years in meditation that an anthill grew up around him. Finally a heavenly presence appeared to him and instructed him to break free from the anthill and to create the Ramayana, or "Rama's Way," a telling in poetic meter of the life of Prince Ram and his wife, Sita. For thousands of years, Valmiki's epic poem has endured as one of the world's most revered sacred stories.

A YOGI is an adept in one form or another of yoga, which

means self-control. There are many schools of yoga, but the chief ones are *Bhakti* (devotion), *Karma* (selfless service), and *Jnana* (wisdom). *Hatha* and *Raja* yoga are detailed systems of using physical postures and breathing techniques to facilitate Communion with God.

Recommended Resources

A tremendous amount of useful information is available to us in this day and age. You cannot possibly read every book or keep up with the work of every worthy organization. It is humbling.

One way to make your choices is by the affinity you feel toward one book or one organization, and then let that one lead you naturally to another. If you feel that sort of affinity toward *It's a Meaningful Life,* then you may wish to write for (or download) the Human Kindness Foundation catalog:

Human Kindness Foundation Catalog (books, audiotapes, videotapes) P.O. Box 2900, Durham, NC 27715. (919) 304-2220 www.humankindness.org

Besides my other books and tapes, the HKF catalog features just a few dozen books, tapes, and videos that we consider precious gems for the spiritual journey, ranging from William Buck's versions of the ancient Mahabharata and Ramayana, to *Finding Freedom: Writings from Death Row* by my friend Jarvis Masters; to *The Gift: Poems* by Hafiz, the Great Sufi master; to the madcap *Tales of a Magic Monastery* by the monk Theophane; to the tiny *Open Secrets* by Rabbi Rami Shapiro.

The materials we carry represent a variety of religious traditions, and are the source of many of the stories or quotes in this present volume. Most are a little hard to find, and that's why we have chosen to make them available. Some of our audiotapes and videotapes feature sacred music or chanting, like Krishna Das's soul-stirring *Pilgrim Heart,* or Tom Key's incredibly talented performance in the video of the stage play *Cotton Patch Gospel.*

Human Kindness Foundation also publishes a free newsletter, *A Little Good News,* three times a year. Many of the chapters in this book had their beginnings as articles in our newsletter. Getting on our newsletter mailing list would also keep you informed of most of our activities, retreats, and my lecture/workshop schedule.

OTHER SOURCES OF INSPIRING AUDIO-TAPES, VIDEOTAPES

Hartley Films
(203) 869-1818
www.hartleyvideos.org

SoundsTrue Catalog
(800) 333-9185
www.soundstrue.com

Mystic Fire Videos
(212) 941-0999
www.mysticfire.com

A FEW GOOD COMMUNITY WEB SITES

The Giraffe Project
www.giraffe.org

Habitat for Humanity
www.habitat.org

Idealist
www.idealist.org
The global clearinghouse of nonprofit and volunteering resources.

The Simple Living Network
www.slnet.com

Volunteer Match
www.volunteermatch.org
In partnership with thousands of local nonprofit organizations VolunteerMatch has built the nation's most comprehensive and up to date database of volunteer opportunities. You can search thousands of volunteer opportunities by zip code, category, and date; then signup instantly by email for those that fit your interest and schedule. Opportunities are posted directly by local organizations to keep the list of walk-a-thons, neighborhood cleanups, tutoring dates, building sites, meal services, and other activities accurate and up to date.

WorldDharma
www.WorldDharma.com

Volunteers for Peace
www.vpf.org

Zen Peacemaker Order
www.peacemakercommunity.org

PUBLICATIONS WITH OPPORTUNITIES FOR SERVICE/VOLUNTEERISM

Alternatives to the Peace Corps: A Directory of Third World and U.S. Volunteer Opportunities edited by Katherine Castro, Phil Lowenthal, Stephanie Tarnoff, Lisa David, 6th edition (Food First Books, 1996). (Out of stock.)

The International Directory of Voluntary Work edited by Victoria Pybus, 6th edition (Vacation-Work, 1997).

International Workcamp Directory, 6th edition (Volunteers for Peace, 1999).

A Student's Guide to Volunteering by Theresa Digeronimo (Career Press, 1995).

Volunteer America: A Comprehensive National Guide to Opportunities for Service, Training, and Work Experinece/With Supplement edited by Harriet Clyde Kipps, 4th edition (Ferguson Publishing, 1997).

Volunteer Vacations by Bill McMillon, 7th edition (Chicago Review Press, 1999).

Index

"abundance and prosperity"
      teachings, problems with,
      152–54
adharma, 249, 250
Adi Granth, 21, 36
adults, as models, 138–39
aging, 52–53, 215–16, 217
alcohol, 28, 149
altruism, 119–20
American culture:
      aging in, 52–53, 215–16, 217
      childrearing in, 92–95, 126,
         136–39, 161–67, 213–14,
         216, 217–18, 249
      community deterioration in,
         121–22, 126, 146, 213–14
      shadow side denied by, 250
      skill development and, 213,
         219–21, 225
      unkindness and discourtesy
         in, 257–58
*Ancient Futures: Learning from
      Ladakh* (Norberg-Hodge),
      26, 214–15

anger, 203–11
      mechanism of, 204, 208
      righteous vs. self-righteous,
         207–8
      working with, 209–11
"anything that can happen"
      mantra, 70–72
appreciation, praise vs., 93–
      94
automobiles, 143
awareness, spiritual, develop-
      ment of, 35–48

Ba'al Shem Tov, 6, 119, 199
Baha'ullah, 153
Beginning to See (Sujata), 9
Be Here Now (Ram Dass), 7,
      37–38
Belleve, Rosabelle, 193, 194
Ben (author's grandfather),
      178–79
Bhagavad Gita, 28–29, 54, 169,
      207
Bhajan, Yogi, 160–61, 162, 166

Bible, *see* New Testament; Old Testament
blame, freeing oneself from, 111–13
blessing, of all humanity, 260–62
Bobby (convict), 240
bodhicitta, 103
Branden, Nathaniel, 94, 100
breathing:
    in meditation, 43–45
    practice of, 15, 190–92
Brhadaranyaka Upanishad, 89
Buck, William, 157
"Buckets of Rain" (Dylan), 195
Buddha, 6, 9, 35, 36, 38, 48, 186, 191, 219
Buddhism, Buddhists, 33, 39, 46, 107–8, 122, 152, 183, 215, 251
    see also Theravadin Buddhism; Tibetan Buddhism; Zen Buddhism

calling, finding of, 168–74
Campbell, Joseph, 15, 170, 171
capable, becoming, 15, 218, 219–27
career:
    fixation on, 177–78
    job vs., 177
Carlebach, Shlomo, 23–24
challenges, facing of, 59–68, 94–95
change, 49–58
    challenge of, 50–51
    as its own reward, 54
    motivations for, 52–53, 55
    necessity for, 50
    responsibility and, 51–52
    self-discipline and, 53–54

    understanding of, 51–55
    vowing to, 56–58
charitable organizations:
    donations to, 133
    volunteers for, 120, 129, 133, 134
children:
    appreciation vs. praise of, 93–94
    autonomy and, 224–25
    negative effects of popular culture on, 160–67, 249
    raising of, 92–95, 126, 136–39, 143–45, 161–67, 212–28, 249
Christ Consciousness, 4
Christianity, Christians, 107, 108, 112, 169, 232, 256
Chronicles of Narnia, The (Lewis), 157
Churchill, Winston, 127
citizenship, as service, 127–34
civilization, 127
    decline of, 128, 135–37
civil rights, 253
Communion, 5, 6, 113–14
community, 5–6, 117–62
    civilizing of, 128–29, 132–33
    consumerism and, 25–27, 136, 146
    deterioration of, in America, 121–22, 126, 146, 213–14
compassion and lovingkindness, 106–14
    "full-time" practitioners of, 108–9
    as humanity's common career, 179
    profundity of, 107
    setting stage for, 110–14

for unfortunate, 254–60
wisdom traditions on, 5, 254
consumerism, 3, 142–43,
154–56, 164, 179, 250
and weakening of commu-
nity, 25–27, 136, 146
see also materialism
control, relinquishing of, 29
criminal justice system, spiritual
mistake of, 255–56
criminals, marginalizing of,
255–58
Cuba, 185–86

Dalai Lama, 32–33, 51, 61–62,
68–69, 108–9, 110,
258–59, 260
Dass, Tulsi, 6–7, 37–38, 108, 154
Davey, H. E., 59
debts, 143, 148
dedicated lives, wisdom traditions on, 169
defeat, humility vs., 73–81
desires, 26–28, 154
self-control over, 28–29
Deuteronomy, Book of, 22
Dhammapada, 152
Dharamsala, India, 107–8
Dharma, 4
dharma, 168, 171, 249, 250, 251
discernment, judgment vs.,
246–53
drugs, 28
Dumbing Us Down (Gatto), 221
Dylan, Bob, 195

Earth, Incorporated, 25–27
Ecclesiastes, Book of, 153, 246
education system, 220–21
ego, moving beyond, 96–97, 98

elders, in American culture,
52–53, 215–16, 217
Elsie (friend), 263–64
enlightenment, realization vs.,
22–23
equanimity, developing of, 67–72
excellence, striving for, 95
Exorcist, The, 161

failures:
humility learned through,
229–31
using of, 232–33
value of, 228–36
faith, 39–40, 67, 69, 71–72
fasting, 16
fear, 26–28, 69
facing of, 28–29, 53, 59–68
"Follow your bliss," 171
Francis of Assisi, Saint, 89, 262
freedom:
unchecked personal choice
vs., 186–88
Western idea of, 186
free will, 28, 67, 68, 83–84, 189

Gandhi, Mohandas K., 76–77,
109, 111, 127, 128, 130,
145, 147, 232
gangs, 94, 214
Gatto, John Taylor, 220–21
Genesis, Book of, 190
Geshe Ben, 33
Gibran, Kahlil, 176–77
Gift, The (Hāfiz), 109–10
gifts, boycotting of, 149
global problems:
seeming insolubility of, 128,
129
tackling of, 133–34

God:
    calling as instilled by, 170,
        171, 172
    name of, in mantras, 78
    nature of, 4, 13, 22
    prayer and relationship with,
        82–87
God-realization, 22–24
Gospel of Ramakrishna, 37
"Grab tightly, let go lightly,"
    154
grace, 23
Griffith, Bede, 39, 110–11
Grossman, David, 162–63

Habitat for Humanity, 134
Hāfiz, 109–10
happiness, 25–34
    barriers to, 26–29
    clarifications and, 30–34
Hasidism, 119, 122, 143
Hau Hu Ching (Lao-Tzu), 14
Hazrat Inayat Khan, 90
Helms, Jesse, 258–59, 260
Hillel, 127
Hinduism, 2, 153, 251, 256
honesty, truth vs., 237–45
Human Kindness Foundation,
    7–8, 232
humility:
    defeat vs., 73–81
    failure and, 229–31
humor, cosmic sense of, 68–69
Huxley, Aldous, 106

individualism, 185–92
Interfaith Order of Communion
    and Community, 7–8
intuition, 241
Islam, 251

Jesus, 6, 9, 75–76, 105, 107,
    108, 109, 118, 124, 130,
    154, 207, 229–30, 231,
    259, 260, 262
job, career vs., 177
John, Gospel of, 21
joy, 29
    self-esteem and, 101, 103
    sorrow and, 29–30
Judaism, 122, 196, 251
judging, discerning vs., 246–53
Jung, Carl Gustav, 37

karma, 67–68
Kindness House, 50
    practices of, 8, 9, 90–91,
        233–34
    talking circles at, 238–39,
        242–43, 266
    visitors and residents of, 8–9,
        237–40, 243
Koran, 152
Krishna, 168, 169, 171, 207
Krishnamurti, Jiddu, 37

Ladakh, childrearing in, 214–15
Lao-Tzu, 14, 38, 124–25
Lewis, C. S., 84, 157
life, as spiritual climb, 60–63
lifestyle:
    civilizing of, 131–32
    consumerist, 3, 25–27, 136,
        142–43, 154–56, 164, 179
    depth vs. shallowness of,
        136–37
Litany of Humility, 98–99
LOVE, love vs., 196–97
Lozoff, Bo, 5, 6–7, 37–38, 51,
    121–22, 177, 185–86,
    223–25, 230–31, 259–60

anger confronted by, 205–7,
   208–9
Dalai Lama visited by, 107–8
housebuilding by, 222–23
lessons from car wreck of,
   73–75
Lozoff, Josh, 8, 164–65,
   170–71, 194, 199,
   223–25, 260
Lozoff, Sita, 5, 6, 8, 37–38, 51,
   63–64, 107–8, 121–22,
   177, 185, 194, 200–201,
   222, 223–25, 230–31,
   237, 259–60, 263

McMillon, Bill, 134
Maggid of Kozhnitz, 119–20
Mahabharata, 13, 152
   see also Bhagavad Gita
mantras, 15, 70–72
   classic, 77–78
   contemporary, 78–80
   practice of, 76–81
Marcus Aurelius, 233
marriage:
   commitment in, 196–97
   God's love and, 197–99
   loss and, 199–201
   as path of service, 193–202
   vows, 197, 202
materialism, 151–59
   conflicts of, 154–55
   sacred reading as counter-
      weight to, 155–59
   wisdom traditions on, 152–53
Matthew, Saint, 259, 260
meals, home-cooked, 150
meditation, 8, 15, 37–48, 172
   benefits of, 48
   classic breath-centered, 40–45

committing to, 41–42
   guided, 46–48
   prayer vs., 84
   purpose of, 37, 38–39, 40
   sitting positions in, 42–43
Meera, Mother, 240
mensch, 215, 220
Michelangelo, 30, 33
Milarepa (Tibetan saint), 256
mindfulness, 16, 122–24
money, relationship to, 151–52
Moses, 72, 96, 172
Moshe of Kobryn, Rabbi, 123
motivation, clarification of,
   30–34
mountain and wind meditation,
   46–48
movies, 161–62, 249, 250
Mr. Rogers' Neighborhood, 164
Muhammad, 6, 72
Murshid Samuel L. Lewis (Sufi
   Sam), 191, 233
music industry, 162, 250

Native Americans, 17, 180, 215
Neem Karoli Baba, 23
New Testament, 13, 21, 49, 75–
   76, 152, 229–30, 233, 262
noise, meditation and, 46–48
Norberg-Hodge, Helena, 26,
   214–15
Norman (resident of Kindness
   House), 237–39, 243
"no-seconds" vow, 16–17
Not Just Stories (Twerski), 119–20

object orientation, process orientation vs., 122–24, 130
Old Testament, 4, 22, 36,
   67–68, 152, 153, 190, 246

On Killing (Grossman), 162–63
Open Secrets (Shapiro), 22
Outward Bound, 59–60, 61, 64

Paul, Saint, 49–50, 256
Peace Pilgrim, 111, 112
Peter, Saint, 229–30, 231, 232, 259
phobias, overcoming of, 63–64
"phony unholy," 108–9
physical exercise, as spiritual practice, 17–18
popular culture, children and, 160–67, 249
pornography, 252–53
possessions, buying and giving away of, 148–49
praise, appreciation vs., 93–94
pranam, 108
prayer, praying, 8, 15, 82–91, 98–99
    genuineness of, 86–87
    meditation vs., 84
    purpose of, 83–84, 85
pride, 92–99
Prine, John, 160
Prison-Ashram Project, 6–7, 232
prisoners, prisons, 6–7, 8, 232, 237–40, 255–58, 259–60
process orientation, object orientation vs., 122–24, 130
Prophet, The (Gibran), 176–77
Psalms, Book of, 4
Pscizche, Rabbi of, 144

radical goodwill, 260–62
Ramakrishna, 6, 83
Ramana Maharshi, 40, 111

Ramayana, 152, 157
reality checking, 237–45
realization, enlightenment vs., 22–23
Reeve, Christopher, 196–97
relationships, 193–202
religions, universal principles of, 5–6, 38, 124, 152–53, 169, 170, 173–74, 249, 250–51, 254–55
right livelihood, 183
right living, 71
right view, 25, 30, 60
right vs. wrong, speaking out on, 248–49, 251, 252–53
Rogers, Fred, 164
Rogers, Murray, 61–62
Romans, Book of, 49
Rūmī, Jalāl al Dīn ar-, 2, 3, 6

sacred, reality of, 2–3, 23, 35–36, 54–55
sacred texts, reading of, 8, 15, 152–53, 155–59
sages and saints, redemption and transformation of, 256
Sanatana Dharma, 2–3
Sat-chit-ananda, 4
seeing, practice in, 103–5
self-discipline, 28–29, 53, 213, 223, 250
self-esteem, 100–105
    fallacies about, 101–2
    joy and, 101, 103
self-esteem, false, 92–99
    childrearing and, 92–96
self-forgetfulness, 103
self-hatred, 28
selfishness, 118

Sermon on the Mount, 75–76, 262

service, practicing of, 117–26
importance of community in, 118, 124–26
nonstop, 120–22
process orientation in, 122–24
pursuit of happiness and, 118–19
self-care and, 119
spiritual practice as counter-balance to, 265–66

Sesame Street, 164

sexuality, 196

Shakespeare, William, 169

Shapiro, Rami, 21–22

sharing, simple living and, 146–47

Shaw, George Bernard, 117, 119

Sherpas, 17

Shunyata, 39

Sikhism, 21, 160–61

silence, practice of, 233–36
longer retreats in, 18, 205–6
on normal days, 8, 9, 234–35
retreat days in, 235–36

simple living, 142–50
childrearing and, 143–45
strategies for, 146–47, 148–50

skills, development of, 213, 215, 218, 219–27

smoking, 28, 51, 149

sorrowful joy, 29–30

"Spanish Pipe Dream" (Prine), 160

spirituality, external, see community

spirituality, internal, see Communion

spiritual laws, 4, 36, 186–87
breaking of, 255–58
of religions, 5–6, 38, 124, 152–53, 169, 170, 173–74, 249, 250–51, 254–55

spiritual practices:
creation of, 13–24
day-to-day life and, 18–20
importance of, 82–83
practice of, 18–24, 265
purpose of, 14–16, 19–21
service and, 265–66
types of, 15, 16–18

spiritual states, objective reality of, 3–4

Stephen, Saint, 112

stopping, 172–74

Story of my Experiment with Truth, The (Gandhi), 147

Story of the Desert Fathers, 113

substance abuse, 28

Sufism, 107, 191

Sujata, 9

"support," 247–48

Table Talk (Rūmī), 2

talking circles, 242–45, 252–54, 266–67
casual conversations vs., 244–45
topics for, 242–44, 267

Talmud, 73

Tao, Taoism, 4, 14

Tao Te Ching (Lao-Tzu), 38

Tashi Deleg, 108

task of life, discerning and ful-filling of, 1–10

technology, enslavement to, 130, 137, 142–43, 146–47

Ted (friend), 263–64, 265
television, 146, 161–67
    learning disabilities and, 163
    limits on watching of, 164–67
Teresa, Mother, 98–99, 101,
    109, 110, 179, 200
Teresa of Avila, 6
Terry (resident of Kindness
    House), 239–40
Theravadin Buddhism, 46
Thich Nhat Hanh, 29, 207,
    237, 244
3HO, 160–61
Tibetan Buddhism, 33, 107–8,
    122
tikkun, 120–22, 170, 172
Timothy, First Book of, 233
Tolstoy, Leo, 193–94
Torah, 73
"tough love," 258
traumas, dealing with, 73–81
truth, honesty vs., 237–45
Tukaram (Hindu saint), 97
Twerski, Benjamin, 119, 143

Universal Mind, 37
Unlocking the Secrets of Aiki-
    Jujitsu (Davey), 59
Upanishads, 89

Valmiki (Hindu sage), 256
values, 135–41, 213, 248–49
    of American culture, 92–95,
        135–41, 142–43, 154,
        155–56, 161–67, 213–14,
        216, 217–18, 249–50
    analysis of, 27–28, 139–41

vanity, 52
video games, as "sociopath simu-
    lators," 163
videos, on saints and sages,
    110–11
violence, popular culture and,
    161–63, 249
Vipassana, 46
vision quest, 180–84
volunteers, 120, 129, 133, 134
Volunteer Vacations (McMillon),
    134
vows, 15, 16–17, 41–42, 56–58,
    65, 111, 166–67, 202

walking, as spiritual practice, 8,
    15, 17
Wang Yang Ming, 10
Wei Wu Wei, 30
We're All Doing Time (Lozoff),
    222, 223
When Harry Met Sally, 137–38
Wilson, Gahan, 68
work:
    meaningful, 175–84
    questions about, 176
    vision quest on, 180–84
world, civilizing of, 127–34
writing, 15, 265

Yellow Lark, Chief, 88
yoga, 8, 15
"You can do hard," 50, 51

Zen Buddhism, 39
Zusya of Hanipol, Rabbi, 172